Author, single mother, journalist, madam and sexpert Samantha X grew up in London, moving to Sydney in 2000 to spend ten years working for Australia's top magazines as a journalist, news editor and beauty director, as well as being a freelance TV producer.

After a few failed relationships, Samantha decided to dip her toe into what she felt was an empowering industry, and became a high-profile escort. In September 2014, Samantha went public and released her first book, *Hooked: The Secrets of a High-Class Call Girl*, and she soon became an inspiration for women and men worldwide wanting to know her secrets in and out of the bedroom.

In 2015, Samantha started Samantha X Angels, a high-class escort agency. She lives by the beach with her two children and two dogs. To find out more, visit:

www.samanthax.com.au
Facebook: @SamanthaXreal
Twitter: @SamanthaX_real
Instagram: @samanthaxreal

BACK ON TOP

CONFESSIONS OF A HIGH-CLASS ESCORT

SAMANTHA X

hachette
AUSTRALIA

Pseudonyms have been used in this book and other details altered where necessary to protect the identity and privacy of people mentioned. While every effort has been made to recall past events accurately, the memories contained within this book are the author's own and may differ from those of others.

[⌐] hachette AUSTRALIA

First published in Australia and New Zealand in 2017
by Hachette Australia
(an imprint of Hachette Australia Pty Limited)
Level 17, 207 Kent Street, Sydney NSW 2000
www.hachette.com.au

National Library of Australia
Cataloguing-in-Publication data:

X, Samantha, author.

Back on top: confessions of a high-class escort / Samantha X.

978 0 7336 3859 6 (paperback)

Escort services
Sex-oriented businesses – Anecdotes
Brothels – New South Wales – Sydney – Anecdotes

Cover design by Luke Causby, Blue Cork Pty Ltd
Cover photographs courtesy of Adobe Stock
Author photograph by Fabrizio Lipari
Typeset in Sabon LT by Kirby Jones
Printed and bound in Great Britain by Clays Ltd, St Ives plc

To all women,
especially sex workers,
who are trying to find their unicorn.

The mass of men lead lives of quiet desperation.

HENRY DAVID THOREAU

CHAPTER 1

AMANDA

Betrayal

He looks at her pleadingly, with fear creeping into his darting eyes.

'But, darling,' he stammers, tentatively trying to snake his arms around her, 'I didn't fuck her, I just wanked on her. Seriously, all I did was blow on her face. I couldn't get hard. You are the only one who makes me hard ...'

Oh my GOD. Did he just say that? Did he just FUCKING say that?

'You fucking arsehole!' she screams, throwing his iPhone at his head, him ducking just in time. 'Wendy West? That pasty fat hooker with the cellulite-splattered stomach? You fucked her two days ago? You piece of shit! You hooker-addicted piece of shit!'

Smash! There goes his shiny photo frame, shattering on the floor. *Bang!* That's his very expensive watch slamming against the wall. *Wallop!* That's her hand slapping his face.

Crash.

There goes her attempt at love.

The cheating bastard was Mr Big, a Melbourne corporate titan who liked the finer things in life. That screaming banshee of a woman? Well, dear reader, that was *me*. Samantha X. High-profile escort, journalist, author, mum and sex industry pioneer (*ahem*). A woman who prides herself on staying true and being empowered – even mentoring other women – yet who, when it comes to her own life, had become a dishevelled bloody mess.

And that was us, fighting in a hotel room in Melbourne. I was fighting with a man I loved who had reduced me to a paranoid, insecure and violent woman, someone I didn't recognise at all, someone who was prepared to put up with being an on-again, off-again girlfriend.

How the fuck did that happen? Before I met Big I was working as an escort, making my own money, doing what the hell I wanted, when the hell I wanted to do it and with whom. Nothing – or no one – made me cry. I had given up a perfectly successful job as a journalist (first in London, where I am from, then in Sydney) to turn men on for money. I loved my new career. In what other job can a single mum with two kids work her own hours making great cash having orgasms?

I was born to do it. I was good at it. And it wasn't just about the money; it never is. The work ticked a few boxes for me personally as well – cuddling, sex and companionship. I didn't want the drama of being emotionally connected to a person. I didn't do relationships. I chose dogs over drama. And now drama seemed to be a huge part of my life. Since meeting Big my life had become a soap opera. *He loves me, he hates me. I love him, I loathe him.* It was exhausting, draining and, with all the crying I did, I swear my Botox never lasted as long.

———

The fight got worse. Oh boy, it got a lot worse.

'You fucking arsehole, you've been fucking other women all along?' I croaked weakly through my tears, my throat turning into a big, fat, sad lump. 'The week I come and see you in Melbourne you wank all over Wendy Fat West? But why, Big, why? Why would you do that to us?'

'Because you make me, Amanda!' he said, not quite convincingly. 'You make me behave this way! I love you, Amanda, but you *make* me turn to other women.'

And so it dragged on. The screaming, yelling, pushing, slamming. Who needed in-room entertainment when you had Mr Big and me as neighbours? I lashed out, scratching and hitting, as he tried to restrain me while managing to delete the reams of evidence on his phone at the same time. It wasn't just Wendy West: more names had popped up on his iPhone less than an hour ago, plus swingers' websites, some naked selfie Snapchat and more. Much more.

To say I felt betrayed didn't do it justice. For the first time in my life I understood what people meant when they said they wanted to vomit out of shock, or that they felt completely and utterly numb. I had to stop myself from either stabbing him to death with the nearest, sharpest weapon I could find or throwing myself on the ground, pleading with him to tell me why. Men pay me thousands to be with them – he had me and he was *still* sleeping with other women.

It had been such a lovely evening. We'd had dinner at a cosy Italian; our favourite type of restaurant. I'd had the vongole – a bit salty, we'd agreed. Big had had the prawns: ripe and succulent with a hint of chilli. He always chose so well. He did everything so well.

And we'd had tickets to the movies – a treat! A proper date! *The Girl on the Train* – I hadn't read the book but the movie looked so good! And who cared anyway, it was two whole delicious hours with the man I loved. Two hours of holding his hands, his large fingers caressing mine, and me nuzzling up to the crease of his shoulder. A whole two hours of me sitting close enough to breathe in his smell, of feeding my addiction to him and that smell. It was his scent I loved the most: expensive, rich, laden with tobacco – not from smoking, he would never do that (except expensive cigars, of course) but from one of his many fragrances. This one I believe was Tom Ford's Tobacco Oud. It was a little strong for me, a little overpowering – reviews said it mimicked the chemical smell of cocaine, but being so handsome and sophisticated, he could pull it off. Big himself was strong and overpowering. He could pull anything off, he really could.

It was cold. Melbourne nights are always cold. The sun did tease during the day, but come evening it could have been the middle of winter again. What do they say about Melbourne – four seasons in one day? It's so true!

As we sauntered slowly back to the hotel, he stopped dead in his tracks in the middle of the footpath. For a second or two, as fellow pedestrians jostled past us, grumbling at our selfish act, it was just Big and me, alone in our warm glow. He pulled me close to him, so close I could take in more divine droplets of his smell.

'Amanda, I love you,' he whispered, cupping my chin and pressing his lips on mine.

For just a few precious moments I was completely and utterly lost in our kiss. This was right. This was passion. This was love. I loved this man and I know he loved me. Well, there you go: Samantha X had found love – fancy that! Even I was surprised.

Arm in arm, we walked back to the hotel, our shoes clicking on the pavement. It was still early – 7 p.m.

'A quick drink?' Big smiled, squeezing my arm.

'Lovely,' I replied, squeezing him back – and then I can't remember now how the unravelling started, it was so silly. We were laughing about something, a private little joke that couples have, as we made our way into the hotel room.

'Let's google it!' he said, grinning as he pressed the buttons on his iPhone, his dear friend, the holder of all information, the keeper of secrets, the protector of lies.

The name we were googling began with a W. And as he pressed W his history popped up – everything he had looked at recently beginning with a W. And two words leapt out, blunt and stark.

Wendy West.

Wait.

What?

Wendy West?

My heart thudded. Actually, I think it missed a beat. Why the fuck was he googling Wendy West? I glanced at him quickly. Had he seen? He was still chuckling at our little joke; he hadn't noticed her name come up.

'Aha – see, darling, there it is. Those lovely Italian plates we like are actually from Wedgwood! Thought as much. Hardly very Italian, is it?'

'Not very,' I whispered, my brain racing. More evidence – I needed more proof. What else? 'What about that lovely hotel we saw in the Qantas magazine, the Signal in Barcelona? Let's have a look at that. Press S.' If anything was going to catch him out, it would surely be the letter 's' for s-e-x. 'S ... I ... G ...'

'Great idea! August, didn't we say? You don't have the kids the first two weeks, do you?'

With his thumb hovering over the letter S, I felt terror. Sheer and utter terror. Maybe it was a mistake. Maybe her name just popped up by mistake ...

As if in slow motion I watched his thumb press softly, so softly, on the letter. *Click!*

S for secrets. S for sex. S for ... SexyChat! Sexy Neighbours! Exchange your nude photos with like-minded swingers! Sarah Smith private escort ... and so it went on. Websites he'd looked at today, yesterday, the day before.

S for ... SHIT. The fucking little shit.

Just like that, in the click of a button, my world caved in. The man I loved clearly loved doing other things with Ws and Ss and god-knows-what other letters of the alphabet behind my stupid, trusting, ignorant back.

The blundering fool was still oblivious to the mess he had just exposed. I quickly snatched the phone out of his hands and scrawled through before he could react.

'Amanda, no!' he yelped, trying to wrestle the phone off me.

'What the fuck, Big,' I whispered, shaking my head, pushing him away. There it was. In black and white, and clear as day. The truth. The websites, the private emails sneakily deleted in his rubbish basket, his considered correspondence to Wendy West.

Dear Wendy ... Just confirming we are still on for 1 p.m. today ... I may be 20 minutes late if that's OK ...

Oh no problem! she had written back (probably filing her nails at the same time). *Can't wait to meet you!*

The date? Two days ago.

Two fucking days ago?

He had been with her two days ago, at lunchtime, while

I was in Melbourne, in our hotel. After I'd flown down from Sydney especially to see him.

I remembered now: we'd had a fight, a little one, but he'd called me at lunchtime to make up. I was on the treadmill at the gym.

'I'm sorry too,' I'd replied, out of breath, my feet pounding on the running belt. 'I love you.'

'Funny way of showing it,' he'd replied quietly. But he was in the office – he could never talk for long. He knew me so well: a fight and it was forgotten. Like a storm, I explode quickly, but moments later it's over and everything seems fresher.

The time? Twelve forty-five. I remembered glancing at the clock, whiling the minutes away, my legs aching. Twelve forty-five ... He must have been on his way to Wendy West; his cock must have been hardening. The excitement and the anticipation of a new woman. Fresh pussy. He'd next called me around two-thirty. After his deceit, his cum probably still leaking from his cheating cock, the smell of another woman on him. His smell on her.

That smell was mine, not hers. It was *mine*. That was *my* fucking smell. Now she could smell him. His smell was probably lingering on every bloody hooker's pillow in Melbourne.

He fucked Wendy the same week he woke me up in the middle of every night to tell me he loved me, the same week he kissed my nose in the morning and brought me coffee in bed. We watched morning TV together as he got dressed for work and had urgent sex just as he was about to leave.

'I can't resist you in your suit!' I'd always say, zipping his fly back up, my pussy still throbbing, wet from the friction of his large, hard cock and his smell, of course, still teasing me as he leaned in to kiss me goodbye.

And I meant it. Big was so handsome. His hair was sandy with the odd grey and, at fifty, he still turned heads. He looked after his skin too. I'd always joke he had better products in his bathroom cabinets than I did – Chanel, Aveda … He had good taste. His suits were Italian, his ties Thomas Pink, his shoes sophisticated leather from a boutique in some trendy suburb where they served you whiskey as you pondered which pair to spend your $1000 on.

Yet all the time in our bubble of love he was planning, plotting, emailing, fucking – sorry, wanking – on other escorts? Paying bloody deposits, for Christ's sake; *planning in advance.*

It wasn't a whim, a one-off. He wasn't drunk in some bar. It was cold, calculating, precise. For someone who was so busy, so stressed at work – who had hushed, hurried conversations with me in the office – he found the time to cheat on me. Like I've said before: men always find the time. I just didn't believe it would happen to *me*.

If that's what he was doing when I was in town, what the fuck was he getting up to when I was back in Sydney?

It wasn't so much the lies, the sneaking around, meticulously taking his phone everywhere with him – even the bathroom – always putting it face down on the dinner table when we were together.

No: it was the hypocrisy. He hated me working and wanted me to give it all up for him. HIM. That lying prick.

The thought of the unfairness of it all made me see red – bright, blood-splattered red. He kept stuttering nervously at me, his mouth moving fast, hollow words trying to justify his actions, but I could no longer hear them.

I hate you I hate you I hate you I hate you. That was all I could hear in my head.

Without thinking, I grabbed the iron that was on the table. I held it to his face and, for a split second, imagined smashing his head in, hard and fast, blood and brain matter splattering all over the walls. Just as I raised my hand to strike, I stopped. What would the headline be?

Samantha X arrested for murder.

Escort mum bludgeons lover to death with iron.

Jesus, my critics would have a field day. I would lose everything. And as for my career? I've not heard of many escorts who put 'murder' down on their list of services (although I know a few who aren't shy of other things, like putting a Valium in the drink of a client who never shuts up). Murdering men in hotel rooms wouldn't exactly be good for business, either. I couldn't see many clients booking me after that. My critics would shake their heads, tutting, 'We knew that woman was bonkers all along.'

Why should I let them win?

Calmly, I put the iron down.

'I need to leave,' I whispered, scared of what I was capable of. 'Let me out.'

'No – I love you, I love you, please don't go, Amanda,' he begged tearfully, barricading me in the suite, blocking the door, pleading with me for forgiveness.

'It's all your fault I fuck hookers!' he wailed, grabbing me by the wrists so tightly he left two big bruises. 'If only you would stop being Samantha, then I wouldn't do it. I wouldn't! I love you, I want to marry you but you won't stop. You torment me, Amanda, you utterly torment me. This is *all your fault.*'

I looked at him with hate and despair, but also with another feeling I had never, ever felt before with him. Relief? Sure, we'd had fights before – awful fights. But this? This was different. This was finally the end.

'Big, you will never, ever be with me again,' I whispered, my turn to be cold now. I looked at him in the eye, not blinking, no emotion. 'You will never kiss me again. You will never feel my warmth or my love again. We will never be together again. I am leaving your life. I am gone.'

And I knew as I uttered those words that it wasn't for show. It wasn't for drama and effect. It wasn't to upset him and make him beg me to come back. I meant every single carefully chosen word.

He stared at me as if he was trying to read my body language. He hadn't seen me like this in a long time: *strong.* It was like how I was when we first met; before I had slowly given him my power, my strength.

He opened his mouth, but there were no words to say to placate me or to make things better. 'Amanda, I can explain,' he said. 'It's not what it looks like. I couldn't fuck her, darling, I just couldn't. Darling, where are you going? Stay here, let's talk. We can work through this ... Amanda ... please ... I am begging you.'

I walked to the door but he didn't stop me this time. As the door quietly clicked shut behind me, I heard him cry out, 'I'm sorry.'

But it was too late.

I know, right? I can see the paradox in the situation: a hooker feeling devastated that her boyfriend was seeing other hookers. Under my very nose! I mean, it was like a scene from a Woody Allen movie. A psychiatrist would rub their hands in glee.

But it hurt. It really hurt, with a pain I had never felt before; with absolute despair. Was this how wives felt when they caught their husbands out? Was this karma? My angels were no doubt looking at this circus shaking their heads, chiming, 'Oh, Amanda, you silly girl, we tried to warn you.' Now I'm not religious per se – I don't believe there is a jolly fat man in the sky – but I do believe sometimes that my guardian angels are looking out for me. And, boy, do I give them some serious headaches.

I flew back to Sydney the next morning with more than a couple of bruises. I was completely and utterly broken. My heart, which was fragile at the best of times, was shattered into a million shards of glass. I couldn't remember the last time I'd let myself become so vulnerable with a man. I was great as Samantha – an escort is an expert at switching the emotion button off. *Click, clack.* But I had stupidly switched it back on for Big and forgotten to turn it off. And look where it got me.

I am so sorry for hurting you …
I love you …

Please forgive me ...

The text messages he sent I just deleted. There was nothing to say. I blocked his number. *Gone.*

I sobbed all the way home on flight QF442, sobbed in the taxi while the bemused taxi driver kept staring into his rear-vision mirror, clearly knowing better than to ask how my morning was going. Then finally, safely back on the doorstep of my Sydney beachside home, sobbing loudly into the licking, smelly faces of my dogs, Rosie and Georgie – the only bloody loyal living creatures I know.

And here I was. Amanda, Samantha, whatever my name was today. Here I was. Alone.

Again.

———

It wasn't how the story was supposed to pan out. For fuck's sake, this wasn't how I was supposed to *be*. Since I wrote my first book, women from all over the globe had been writing to me in droves asking my secrets for how to be confident in and out of the bedroom, or how to be strong and successful, how to become an escort or more sexually charged.

You're my idol, they'd write, or *I want to be like you.* And this one: *I'll never be like you, Samantha, so strong, so confident ...*

Pah! Look at me!

I was a fraud, an absolute bloody joke.

I felt like a conwoman writing back to them, shrilly rattling off lines like, 'Stay true! Stay strong!' when really I was struggling to even see my own self-worth.

Those fucking words: *Stay true*. My tagline. My motto. Words I tried to live by. Words I'd had inked on the inside of my left wrist a few years earlier when I'd been in Los Angeles, about to appear as a guest on a talk show called *The Doctors*. 'Whoa! Go, girlfriend!' the audience had shouted, women fist-pumping for me. Strong woman! Brave woman!

What a load of crap. It was that same wrist Mr Big had grabbed, leaving an angry-looking bruise that was changing colour each day; a reminder of that awful night.

Stay true ...

Words I firmly believed in when I was being slammed in the media for outing myself publicly. *Stay true. Believe in yourself. Don't be ashamed of who you are. Own it, girlfriend!* And now look at me. What a joke I'd become.

How could I mentor women when I couldn't even look myself in the mirror?

How could I tell women to leave their abusive husbands? I didn't leave. I still loved him. After all, I wasn't an easy woman ... or so he kept telling me.

And, even more importantly, how the bloody hell had it come to this?

A few days later, fifty red roses turned up with a grovelling note: *Sorry I've been a prick. I'm not perfect but I love and care for you dearly and always. Mr Big.*

I would never throw flowers out – they're living creatures – so instead I kept them in the hallway where I couldn't see them all the time. Just a reminder as I walked into my house that only guilty, lying pricks send flowers.

He knew he'd been blocked, so he once tried calling me from his office line.

'Amanda.'

I hung up quickly. Then blocked that number too.

He wrote me rambling emails about how much he loved me, how sorry he was, how I had hurt him too, how we could make it work.

I'm asking for one more chance, I know our connection is special.

Then: *I love you, I can't live without you.*

Then: *Fuck, you really hate me, don't you?*

'Amanda, you absolutely cannot reply,' my best friend Tab would say tersely when I would call her, crying, at least twice a day. 'You have to get rid of him for good. Replying is giving him attention.'

Tab had been on the other end of the phone too many times now, trying to stem my tears. If anyone was sick and tired of our fights, it was Tab. She made no secret about not liking Big; she had witnessed my distress far too often. She'd even banned him from her home.

'He is not welcome here anymore,' she'd said quietly months ago, after another fight.

Every news article, every blog on 'How to Leave a Narcissist' she'd email to me. *Great story in the Financial Review* were her desperate words, secretly pleading for me to read an article I would otherwise not look at.

I wouldn't always listen to her. She had what I sometimes craved: simple domesticity. She had the husband, the home, the family. She had a wonderful mother, Veronica, who had mothered me better in the fifteen years I'd known her than I'd ever been mothered before. Tab got to go to bed with someone she loved and wake up with him (unless he was snoring, in which case she'd kick him out to the spare room). Just normal stuff.

Me, I always promised I would never live with a man again. But Big had given me a glimpse of what a relationship was like and I'd realised what I had been missing. He went to Country Road to buy me nice plates. He spent a fortune in Le Creuset for pots and pans for my house. He'd pay for me and my kids to go to Hawaii; of course, he never came with us – what could he tell his friends and family? I was a secret. No one knew. Now no one would ever know, because we were done.

Except sometimes when I was feeling sad, weak and lonely, I would type a few words – *Leave me alone, there is nothing to say* – just to secretly feel a pulse of connection by flicking him an email.

Or once I wrote this, after a series of persistent emails from him: *Leave me ALONE, Big. I am on my way to meet a client, a kind, decent man, not a cheating prick like you.*

That clearly rattled him, as I knew it would, and the nastiness came out once again: his true colours. He just couldn't help himself.

I'm fucking a 29-year-old tonight. She's begging me for it. I will parade her at our hotel so everyone can see her.

Delete.

Then, more.

You're nothing but a whore. I feel sorry for you and anyone who comes into your path. You're a cold-hearted bitch, a gold digger, a slut … and so it continued.

Ignored. Then deleted. An ageing businessman with a master's degree in Politics was behaving like this? It beggared belief.

But it hurt. It really hurt. I cried for a few weeks, maybe more. I cried with friends, over the phone, in cafes. I cried in yoga. I cried in my F45 circuit class as I was straining to lift more than a measly five kilos. I cried in the school playground. I cried to my counsellor, Doris.

'He's a fucking arsehole,' I wept one day, blowing my nose into tissues.

She looked at me with concern clear in her pretty mascaraed eyes. For two long years she had listened to me bleat on about my issues with Big. Two long years she'd had to hand me tissues and shake her head sadly. Two long years.

'Yes, Amanda,' she said. 'It is very upsetting for you, I can see.' And as she stared at me, she was probably secretly thanking my angels who were high-fiving each other: once and for all, they had manifested the end.

One day, weeks earlier, I had been walking home past my favourite Italian restaurant. I glanced through the window and saw my friend Cristian working there.

'Cristian!' I called out, and he came to me, and I cried in his arms.

'Another bad fight?' he asked, looking at the bruises on my wrists. 'Come on, Amanda, give me his number. I want to give him a message, Italian-style. He will be sleeping with the fishes soon.'

My answer was *no*, of course – no message needed. My silence was deafening enough as it was. But, yes. Bruises. Fighting had become part of our relationship. He never hit me, never raised his hand. Instead, that night at the hotel in Melbourne, I had scratched and lashed out more than he had. But he was dominant and forceful. He had grabbed me to stop me hitting him. And the most repulsive thing I felt when we were fighting? I still wanted him.

'You are not the same strong woman I met two years ago,' my business partner, Vanessa, said to me gently a few days later, after another one of our meetings ended up with me sniffling into my green tea, hot tears falling into even hotter water.

Ah. Well, a lot can happen in two years, can't it?

Two years ago I was confidently looking into the TV cameras of Channel Seven's *Sunday Night* show, outing myself as the journalist turned high-class escort. Not just that, I was an author too, releasing my first book, *Hooked*, my tell-all memoir of how, at the age of thirty-seven, with two kids and one separation, I had left my nine-to-five job as a successful magazine writer to pursue sex work – and how I bloody loved it. I had a 'fuck you' attitude about my 'fuck me' job, and held no shame in working in what I believed – and still believe – to be an empowering and exciting industry.

Oh, don't get me wrong: I had my haters. Mostly a handful of other escorts who had brave voices behind their keyboards as they spouted vitriol about other women – and they had a different victim every week. But I didn't care. I didn't even read what they wrote. I don't have time for bullies. What's the saying – social media gives idiots a voice? A bit like a fly buzzing around your ear. Soon enough, they shuffle on like a herd of dumb sheep. And besides, I was too busy to pay attention most of the time.

I was labelled by the press as one of Australia's most high-profile escorts and was a regular contributor to newspapers, TV and radio, plus speaking at events.

'Really, do people still want to hear my story?' I'd ask Vanessa after she would tell me such-and-such from so-and-so wanted to interview me. I was a journalist turned escort, my first book was now two years old. Was it still so fascinating?

'Yes!' she would always snap back with a smile. 'Just because you are bored of talking about it, that doesn't mean people are bored of hearing it! People will always be fascinated by the sex industry and you!'

And she was right. One adjective men always used to describe me when they met me was 'intriguing', and the controversial opinion pieces I wrote for newspapers and websites were always among the most-read and commented on by the public. Some of the comments were supportive, others were just plain nasty or completely pointless. *Is it just me or is Samantha X looking more and more like a man?* was one favourite of mine. Another: *Am I the only one who thinks Samantha X is getting a bit plump?* Ouch, that one hurt. Plump? I mean, who the hell says 'plump' these days? And I've yet to meet a man who looks like me, but if I do, he can start seeing my clients instead of me.

During those two years I was overwhelmed by women writing to me in their thousands, wanting to be escorts, so I thought that the most obvious thing to do would be to set up my own (award-winning) escort agency, Samantha X Angels. I handpicked women of all shapes, sizes and ages as escorts, from a 61-year-old granny to a 21-year-old law student. It wasn't just beauty I was looking for but compassion, maturity and kindness. And, yes, I was still escorting.

Men from all around the world still wanted to spend time with me, even though I was no spring chicken. I always said that as long as men were dumb enough to pay my fees, I would be smart enough to take the payment.

And I did love my job — more so my clients — when I did it. Since meeting Big, though, I'd cut down on my work. I'd stopped seeing as many clients. I still had my regulars, still drank Champagne, nibbled on caviar, and was taken on luxury overseas trips First Class. But I wasn't driven enough to be the richest, busiest girl in town: I was in love with Big.

I had a handful of successful businessmen as companions and rarely saw new clients. Despite my rates being set at $1100 for one hour, I hardly ever saw clients for one hour. It was weekends away and week-long trips, not quick frissons in hotel rooms (sadly). I hardly had sex anymore! I probably dealt with women wanting to be escorts more than I saw men. But I had a handful of regulars who I really liked. Nice, kind, easy men that I wouldn't just have sex with. I'd have mini-relationships with them – professional, of course, no commitment involved. Sex, as usual, was bottom of the list. It was not why they were there. They knew they were going to get it, so why rush it? (And, believe me, it rarely lasted very long.) Bookings were drawn out with a nice meal, a bottle of wine, or perhaps a few hours in a hotel room watching a movie. And talking. Boy, was there a lot of taking. Mostly from them. About their lives, their marriages, their failings.

I also had a great team of loyal and talented people around me in business. Some wonderful ladies who escorted for me – the Angels. And Vanessa. Thank god for Vanessa.

Having read my first book on her honeymoon, Vanessa tracked me down with an impressive email about how she could take my brand places and how she believed in what I was doing. Conservative, petite, with feisty Italian fire, married to her softly spoken soulmate, Daniel, and with an impressive career in film marketing, she believed in me. Vanessa coming into my life was one of the best things to happen to me. She encouraged me to ride the wave of my success and to build my brand. And build it she did. When she took over, our expenses dropped and our income grew. Everything within the agency clicked into place finally – and it was all due to Vanessa. I was happy to be the face of the agency, to handpick and train girls and be the gatekeeper to all clients – but Vanessa was the linchpin. She kept us moving.

I loved her family too: her sweet Italian parents were just as kind to me as they were to her; kinder than mine were. Vanessa's success in making Samantha a success made them very proud indeed. We exchanged cards at Christmas and her mum even baked me traditional Italian lemon biscuits. I hadn't spoken to my parents in three years; their anger and hurt – and mine – were too deep.

By this stage I was supposed to be pushing myself to be bigger, better, more successful. I was supposed to be selling sex, fantasy and female empowerment. So how the hell had my life come to this – snivelling into a crumpled tissue, my head buried in my soggy pillow, crying about the fact that I, a once fiercely strong woman, was now too beaten, too fragile, to summon up any strength or self-belief? I felt I'd let Vanessa down. She'd worked tirelessly to get me sponsorships and publicity, yet my heart was no longer in it. Hadn't been for over a year or so – since meeting Big. I had surrendered my power to a man and look where it had got me. What the fuck was I thinking? How could a strong woman get caught in such a toxic relationship?

'But I love him!' I wailed to Tab.

'You do *not* love him, Amanda, you love the idea of him,' was always her response.

And Vanessa wanted better for me. I was not the same woman now. I was a victim.

When did that happen? Samantha was never a victim. She was never weak. I started to flick through my first book, amazed at how strong I sounded then. Who the hell was she? Where was that woman now? Because I no longer knew.

And somewhere deep, really deep inside of me, a little flame started to burn, small but fierce. Not self-pity or sadness, but an intense yellow flickering flame: anger. Determination.

It was time Samantha came back.

CHAPTER 2

SAMANTHA

The doctors

He was too skinny for my liking but that didn't matter. Any escort will tell you it makes no difference at all what clients look like: fat, thin, bald, six toes, a fake ear. Yes, I had one of those once. He twisted off his artificial ear and laid it on the glass of the table, just before he ate my pussy out. I don't know what was worse: staring at his tragic plastic ear lying on the glass table like a dismal souvenir, or his eager head bobbing up and down between my legs, with the safety pin that was holding his floppy ear skin together rubbing against my thigh.

I digress.

My point is that as long as the client is a nice person and has a kind heart, you can find the good in anyone. That doesn't mean, of course, that you are desperate to suck his dick, but that's another thing an escort will tell you: the sex is the easy part. It's the mental bit – the talking, more so the listening – and the constant emotional support you give a client that are more demanding than penis-in-vagina. The sex is actually time to zone out a bit; it can be terribly mentally draining listening to a handful of stories a day from a handful of different men. Sometimes, quite frankly, giving them a blow job is a welcome relief; a bit of a distraction. A cock is a cock is a cock after all, whether it's attached to a male model or an overweight accountant. And they are all pretty much the same in that department. I've yet to see a disgusting cock, to be honest – unless it's attached to a person with a mean heart.

Now to another client: he was a doctor, a well-established one. The kind who travelled the world giving lectures to young, eager medical professionals on his area of expertise. His eyes momentarily lit up as he described the cities he loved: New York, London ... but Singapore was his favourite – such a lovely 'clean' city, such 'clean' hotels.

I raised an eyebrow. Clean? That was a funny adjective when describing a hotel, wasn't it? I mean, don't you take it for granted that hotels are clean?

But, clearly, clean was a big thing for him – he even looked clean, with a healthy, glowing, sensible face hiding behind shiny (clean) glasses. His skin was freshly exfoliated, his hair grey and thin, his features pointy, and his suit was a crisp navy design with a purple handkerchief proudly poking out of the pocket. It was his nervousness that I noticed most.

'Would you like a drink, a glass of pinot perhaps?' I asked him, beckoning him to the cream-coloured sofa. He checked the sofa before brushing it with his hands, as if wiping off some imaginary dirt. I squinted at where he was brushing. There was nothing there. Maybe just nerves?

'Have you seen an escort before?' I asked, pouring his wine before sitting next to him. That line was always a good icebreaker.

Was it my imagination or did he inch away slightly? Embarrassed, I moved away from him too. Rule number 4001: always mirror the client. Was I too close? Invading his personal space? *Never mind, don't take it to heart*, I told myself. It wasn't often I couldn't work a client out. It rarely happened that I couldn't deduce their personalities and match accordingly when I was with them. But this one had me stumped. A bit like a car that couldn't quite get into gear, *we* couldn't quite get into gear.

'Er, yes, yes, I did once,' he stammered, checking the glass before he drank from it. *For god's sake,* I thought, irritated now. This is a five-star hotel, not a dingy motel. I was one of Australia's most expensive escorts. Did he really think I would be giving him pinot in a dirty wine glass?

'But it didn't end well, I'm afraid ...' he said, trailing off, his eyes glassy, as if he was being transported back to some traumatic event.

'Oh?' I replied, snapping out of my little sulk. I always loved hearing stories of other escorts. It's good to find out how others behave, to learn the secrets from inside their hotel rooms. Not many escorts give away their secrets, good or bad – it was the clients who blabbed, and I would devour their stories eagerly. *Aha, she does it like that, does she!* Or, more likely: *she gives excellent deep throat, does she? And squirts on demand? Shit. Mental note: must try harder.*

'She gave me crabs!' he announced, spitting the words out. 'It was quite awful, Samantha! I was itching for days. I had no idea what was wrong until I saw this little creature jumping around in my pubic hair. My wife nearly caught me out when she asked why I was scratching so much. I had to shave off all my hair and I looked like a fourteen-year-old boy down there. It was a very traumatic experience – one I don't wish to repeat. It took me years to recover from the shock and I haven't seen an escort since.'

I blinked, looking at him. What a funny little man. I swear he was about to cry. I was surprised a sex worker had passed on crabs, though – we are such clean little creatures, so safe. Do men really think we would be in the business and actually make money if we were carrying around diseases and scratching our stinky, lice-ridden vaginas every five minutes?

But more shocking was the fact that this doctor, who probably had seen many deaths and terrible illnesses, had watched so many bodies grapple for their final gasp of oxygen, was so traumatised by catching crabs. Surely his experience with dying people made him put minor things like that into perspective? Those dastardly critters were hardly a death sentence. Annoying, sure; dangerous, even, that his unsuspecting wife might have caught them. But let's get real: no one died.

'Oh, that's awful!' I exclaimed, feigning horror and making all the right sympathetic noises. 'How terrible for you – how traumatic. I can assure you that I do not have crabs or any other sexually transmitted disease.'

'Can you?' he interrupted, a surge of panic in his voice. 'Can you, Samantha? You don't, do you? I just would hate to go through that again. Excuse me, Samantha, I must use your bathroom. May I?'

And with that he leapt up and practically ran to the bathroom. I am not even sure he used the toilet but I did hear the taps go on full blast – perhaps he was washing his hands.

I was annoyed now. It was going to be a very long two hours. I mean, if he was so paranoid about catching something from a woman, surely the safest thing to do was to not see other women?

No, I thought, scratching my head, *he couldn't resist it though, could he? They just can't help themselves. These men, they think with their cocks first, head second.* Smiling now, I scratched my head again. And then again. Why on earth was I so itchy?

Probably sympathy pains! I thought, giving my scalp one final scratch before Dr OCD tentatively came back to the bedroom.

'Now, darling,' I purred sexily, patting the bed, 'why don't you make yourself more comfortable while I freshen up in the bathroom ...'

Just as I closed the bathroom door I saw him nervously checking the sheets, brushing the pillows – no doubt wiping away imaginary germs – before climbing inside. He was well and truly irritating me now.

I don't suppose he'll go down on me, what with all my germs, I thought, sitting on the loo.

How the hell was I supposed to have sex with someone who was so paranoid about germs? I mean, seriously. He was with the best. What did he think he was going to catch – Samantha Fever? He wouldn't be the first!

I chuckled to myself as I scratched my head. And again. This time just behind my ears. Behind my ears? *My ears?*

Jesus Fucking Christ. Surely not ... I didn't, did I?

I quickly leapt off mid-pee and raced to the mirror with my G-string halfway down my legs. Frantically I threw my head to one side and raked my fingers through my hair. *Oh my god oh my god oh my GOD.* I saw one, darting in and out of my hair follicles, a big fat creature with a big fat belly full of my blood. I had nits. I had fucking nits.

My mind raced back to a few days earlier, to when I was at home, applying nit treatment on my daughter for the third time in just as many months.

'Darling, I am going to have to wash my pillows now because you've been sleeping with me! Maybe you'll sleep in your own bed now!' I teased her gently, combing the gooey lotion through her soft, silky hair.

But I didn't wash them, did I? I didn't wash them, and now I had bloody nits.

What the hell was I going to do? My hair was long and loose. Maybe if I put it up in a ponytail the nits would curl up and go to sleep for a few hours?

Jesus. They didn't look different to crabs. What if one escaped and somehow ended up on my pussy and then I gave him nits on his pubes ...? I shuddered, feeling sick. It wasn't even worth thinking about. He'd probably throw himself off the Sydney Harbour Bridge, but not before writing a review about how Samantha gave him NITS. The mean ones (and there's always a few) would no doubt revel in this and bitch about me behind my back – and on social media – making sure *everyone* knew Samantha had crawly things. My business and my reputation would be ruined. I would be a laughing stock.

No. It would be fine. I was being dramatic – 'catastrophic', as Doris, my counsellor, always called me. It was just a few nits and adults really couldn't pass them on to each other anyway, could they? *Come on, Samantha – get a grip.*

'Now, handsome,' I breathed, faking confidence and surety, walking back into the bedroom and climbing under the sheets. 'Maybe you can give me a quick check-up down there ...' Cheekily I opened my legs for him.

The sex was quick and mechanical, on both our parts. I was paranoid about my head going anywhere near him and he would have been paranoid that I was going to give him every single disease in his medical dictionary. It was a few desperate thrusts with a carefully implemented and meticulously constructed condom (he had brought his own – of course. Extra strong, naturally).

'Gosh, doctor,' I said breathily a few moments later, finishing up. 'You were fantastic – such a strong, hard, *clean* cock.' I knew his ears would prick up at the word 'clean' and no doubt it made him feel very happy indeed.

He smiled. 'Thank you, Samantha,' he laughed, 'for putting me at ease.'

We kissed and cuddled for a while longer; he was quite a different man once he had relaxed and trusted that I wasn't some disease-ridden fleabag. And, funnily enough, my head had stopped itching. Maybe I had imagined I saw a nit.

'Well, Samantha, that was truly a lovely experience,' he said, getting up and kissing me on my forehead. 'I would love to see you again – more often, if that's okay. I've found someone I can trust. It was hard for me; I was scared before meeting you. Scared I'd catch something again. But thank you. Thank you for making me trust you.'

I smiled. Maybe I really was the best in this game! Maybe I did have a special knack for making men feel at ease, for making them feel safe.

As I watched the doctor get dressed – carefully, of course, shaking out any kind of dust that had settled on his fine suit – he did something that made me freeze.

He scratched his head.

Nah – just a silly head scratch, I thought. Everyone scratches their head. I bet you're doing it now just reading this! It's catching!

But he did it again. Another scratch, harder this time. He looked perplexed, checked himself in the mirror, squinting at his reflection, peering at the top of his head.

'Oh, you are most welcome!' I stammered, grabbing his shoes and almost throwing them into his hands, then shoving his jacket at him. 'Goodness, doctor, is that the time?' And before he could say a proper goodbye, I ushered him from the bedroom and out the front door, to his confusion.

'Sorry – next client due,' I said urgently. 'I would never usually be in such a rush like this but I would simply hate for you two to meet.' I went to shut the door, leaving him ruffled and bemused. 'Bye, doctor, have a nice day.'

'Samantha?' he said, his hand reaching up to his head in what looked like slow motion.

'The pleasure,' I whispered as I shut the door, 'was all mine ...'

Funnily enough, I haven't seen him since.

———

Now, while we're on the subject of doctors, I have to tell you about one of my favourite clients. Let's call him Professor

Doodle from Victoria. Clearly that isn't his real name, but I can't and won't name anyone in my book. Why call them by their real names – like boring old John or Steve – when I can make up something amusing like Professor Doodle? I don't need to identify them and it would cause more than a ball ache for the 'guilty'. Especially Professor Doodle. You see, a few years back his wife had caught him out shagging hookers.

'Just one,' he was always quick to tell me. 'It was just one, Samantha. She found the hotel receipt in my trouser suit.' I know, right! What an old-fashioned mistake! A rookie error! But she furiously threw the receipt under his nose and, being a terrible liar and petrified he would end up under the floorboards, he 'confessed all'. Well, when I say 'all', I mean all in men's terms. A half-truth. Let's call it an 'economy of the truth'.

The professor – who was well and truly in his sixties – confessed to his furious wife that he had met up with one 'lady', once, in a hotel room for one tiny little hour and they had sat down on the bed fully clothed and talked. There had been zero physical intimacy, he told her, because he felt so guilty that he 'failed to get an erection'.

If she believed that, she would also believe in little green men running around on Mars. But she chose to believe him, as most women do. It's easier that way sometimes, isn't it?

What Professor Doodle had omitted to mention to his wife was that there had been several other hookers before that one and several more after her. He never booked for just one hour and he had been seeing hookers for decades. And as for the limp-dick line? A few clients have told me they've used it on their wives if and when caught – and I am telling you now that it's bullshit. It certainly was in the professor's case. And besides, he could write himself prescriptions for Viagra until the cows came home, so it was an issue he could easily solve. In fact, the professor's only issue in the trouser department was carelessly leaving loose hotel receipts lying around in pockets.

Anyway, the professor and his wife had a few sessions of excruciatingly embarrassing therapy (as he called it) and he promised the audience of his furious foot-tapping wife and the matronly open-toed-sandal-wearing counsellor (who probably knew he was talking bollocks) that he would never, ever enlist the services of a PROSTITUTE ever again and could his wife please find it in her generous heart to forgive him.

'I was secretly hoping my wife would understand and give me permission to see the odd escort,' he told me, 'but she wouldn't have any of it.'

Funny that, doc! Silly, sweet man. Nope, his wife didn't give him permission so he stopped for a while – until the heat was off, as they all do. I can't imagine women out there giving their husbands permission to cheat, because it *is* cheating, isn't it?

Unsurprisingly, once the dust had settled, and his unloved cock started twitching again, Professor Doodle went back to clicking on the usual websites until he found someone else he liked the look of: me.

Now, look: he was not a terrible person and partner, and I was certainly not contributing to the demise of his marriage. I urge you to think about this: Professor Doodle loved his wife. They did nice things together, like travel the world three times a year, and hike across Tasmania in their sensible hiking boots and wet-weather jackets, and they shared many things, like their love for politics and what he called 'issues of social justice'. He adored the fact that his wife was the first to head up a political rally or fly to Europe to hear a poetry recital.

Professor Doodle knew the only thing I would protest about was whether my Champagne was too sweet or if my steak was overdone. He liked to hold my hand when we had meals out together – French was his favourite cuisine. (It amazes me that these men don't worry about getting caught out again. Or maybe they want to be caught?) He liked picking me up in his new Mercedes and he asked me not to wear knickers. But, most of all, I think he liked the text messages he fired off to me when his wife went to bed at 8 p.m. I'd be putting the kids to bed when I'd get something like this: *Wife asleep!! Cooked lamb roast tonight!!! Suppose you are out with your friends!!!* or *Wife in bed again!! Watching a fascinating documentary about politics in Bulgaria!! BBC news channel!!!* (It doesn't matter how educated the gentleman is, they will still overindulge in an exclamation mark or three.)

However, the best bloody thing about Professor Doodle was that he was a doctor. And anyone who knows me well knows that in addition to being an escort, mum, author and agency boss, I am the world's worst (or best) hypochondriac. Even in the middle of writing the first three chapters of this book, I took myself off to hospital to check that the stress of my deadlines hadn't given me a heart attack.

'I think you're going to live. Your heart is fine,' the doctor murmured, peering at the X-ray he'd just taken of my chest. I was shocked he could see past the enormous amount of silicone, to be honest. Actually, I think he was *only* looking at my tits.

'Oh, that's a relief, doctor, thank you.' I smiled weakly. Any hypochondriac will tell you of the very slight – and I mean *very* slight – momentary feeling of disappointment when you realise you can't stay in hospital for a few nights and have cups of tea made for you and lots of nice drugs to wash away your emotional pain. That you actually can't run away from your life.

So I absolutely loved Professor Doodle, my personal medical consultant.

Doc, do you think I've got a tumour? I texted him once after a particularly bad headache.

He wrote back with a checklist of symptoms before writing: *No. Take some Panadol and go to bed.* And that he would check on me in the morning.

'Can you just have a quick listen to my heart?' I asked once as he lay on top of me with his hard cock sliding in and out of my pussy. 'I worry I've got cardiac arrhythmia. My heart keeps palpitating really weirdly.'

He stopped for a second and put his head to my heaving breast before pushing his cock into me again.

'Sounds fine to me, Samantha,' he panted, bucking up and down on my sweaty body.

Another time: *Doc, can people die from hangovers?* I texted earnestly. And I was serious. I was panicking that my heart was about to give up on me and that the pounding headache I was feeling would trigger a stroke. This was after just three – yes, just three – Champagne cocktails, I might add, at some bar in Canberra where the teenaged barman confessed, just as I drained the last drops of my third glass, that he had accidentally tripled the measure of spirits in each drink. I was so drunk by then I couldn't even focus on his acne, but I remember laughing triumphantly and trying to high-five him. Extra-strong drinks – what a hero!

But the next day I wanted to wring his scrawny, spotty neck. I had spent the morning with my legs elevated against the hotel room wall, trying unsuccessfully not to (a) vomit and (b) panic about dying alone in some hotel room, with no one finding my body until the cleaners came in. And I really, really didn't want to be found dead in Canberra. LA, New York, London, Paris – even Melbourne – sure. But Canberra? It was hardly going to be a glamorous write-up in the papers: *Oh that escort woman Samantha X? She was found dead ... in CANBERRA of all places ... snigger snigger ...*

Are you in Canberra? Professor Doodle wrote back. *I'm at a conference here too. RU OK?*

No. I'm dying.

Meet you in your hotel? Coffee?

You're joking aren't U? Hangover.

I'll write you a prescription.

My eyes lit up. Of course he could write me a prescription! Why the hell hadn't I thought of that before? God, I love my clients.

So I dragged myself to the hotel lobby, where Professor Doodle was waiting for me in his summer shorts and sandals, carrying a tan leather manbag.

'You know I could get into lots of trouble doing this,' he said, smiling, scribbling a note on a scrappy sheet of paper to prescribe anti-nausea drugs. 'There's a Priceline up the road. Go and get them now and take one, and I'll order your coffee.'

'But I can't read your writing,' I protested weakly, squinting at the spidery words.

'I know. That's how the pharmacist will know it's authentic.'

The pharmacist raised an eyebrow when I passed him the piece of paper and was clearly straining to read the note. He even had to fetch his spectacles.

'Ah! That's better!' he chimed, and off he marched to fetch whatever magic medication the professor had ordered me. And it *was* magic.

One tiny white pill later and my hangover disappeared in less than ten minutes. And, no, I can't remember the name of the drug – I know that's what you're all wanting. But I carry it on trips just in case.

Once I had to cancel all my bookings due to the fact I had a tiny cold sore on my lip. Every single client was thankful I was honest about it and rebooked for another time. Professor Doodle? *Don't worry about it – see you at 3 p.m.* was his response. Out of everyone, the only man who wasn't scared of a cold sore was the doctor.

Later he told me – after he had finished licking my pussy – that most people had the cold sore virus, and it was his gain and the other men's loss that they didn't see me that day.

All of this was why I loved Professor Doodle. He had class, sophistication, common sense and, best of all, drugs. He was a doctor and saved lives, and cured terrible diseases like ... hangovers. I also loved him because he had flaws like all of us. He was a naughty boy, and despite getting caught once, he didn't stop doing it again.

Now, a message to the wives out there: you think because you've caught them out, they stop? Sorry, but they don't stop just because you tell them to. Sure, they will make all the right noises and go to counselling; they will go through the motions of sorrow and guilt, begging for forgiveness and promising that they will never, ever seek the services of a paid companion ever again. But in my experience – and I can only ever talk about my experience – they all come back to me when the coast is clear.

One regular client once called me nervously to tell me that his wife had just found all our text messages synced on the iPad he'd bought her for Christmas (Apple, seriously, what were you thinking?) and he could never see me again.

'Oh shit, James,' I said, 'I am so sorry. I completely understand and I wish you the very best.'

I mean, what else was I supposed to say? I felt a huge surge of guilt that some woman somewhere in Australia was going through heartache and I was involved in it. If only she knew that I wasn't emotionally invested in her husband at all. If only wives knew that escorts have zero interest – and I mean *zero* interest – in trying to steal their husbands.

'Samantha, I shall miss you but I need to give my marriage a go,' he managed to get out in response.

Good luck, I thought. They hadn't had sex in almost ten years; they were both pushing sixty, with separate beds and different lives. Now she was threatening to take most of his money and to tell their kids because he had looked elsewhere for intimacy? Get real, woman. Everyone deserves to be touched. Everyone deserves to be loved – even if it is just for an hour or two. The whole thing made me cross. Okay, maybe seeking escorts isn't the best way to deal with your marriage issues – I'm a big believer in communication first – but, god, are some women so delusional that they think their husbands can live in a sexless marriage?

Yes, they have porn, but sometimes a laptop isn't the only thing you want to keep you warm at night. I've had men tell me that scrolling through X-rated websites makes them feel more lonely than ever. Humans need human touch. Is that such a crime? At least he wasn't shagging the secretary.

'She may call you,' James went on, 'but I've told her I've only seen you once and that we just talked. I couldn't get it up – that's what I told her.'

'Okay.' For fuck's sake. Here we go, more bullshit. An escort's nightmare: *My wife may call you.*

So I won't tell her about the time you booked me and my Angel and watched eagerly as I licked her pussy? I won't tell her about the time you booked me three times in one week while your wife was at the tennis?

But it does beg the question: what would I say to her? My instinct has always been to tell the truth. I always side with women. I am a girls' girl. My friends are female. I prefer female company. Don't get me wrong, I need men – but I crave female relationships.

We all know what men are like, don't we? One escort I know had this dilemma: a very upset young wife called her once, pleading with her to tell the truth about whether her husband had seen said escort on a certain date. The wife had found her number on their phone bill and was fixated on this certain date.

'She had such desperation in her voice that my heart went out to her,' the escort told me. 'So I told her the truth.

I went through my diary and told her, yeah, that sounds about right. Turns out the fucking bastard saw me two hours before their first baby was born.'

I fretted about my dilemma for a few days, but James's wife never called. Part of me did want to talk to her, though, woman to woman, and tell her the truth: 'Look, Mrs Smith, your husband loves you very much but needs to occasionally have sex. Maybe not once a week, but once a year would be nice. Could you even manage twice? He comes to me because the intimacy has gone in your marriage. You can't expect him not to find it elsewhere.'

I wondered how she would have reacted. How would you react? With the sinking realisation that while she may have a wonderful relationship, wonderful companionship – with her husband, her best friend – that that simply is not enough for men? Yes, it is wonderful you play golf together, or you both have a fascination for medieval churches in Ireland, or that you both look forward to when your eldest son visits from uni. But that simply is not enough for men. The truth hurts sometimes – actually, most of the time. That I know for sure. But the cold truth, ladies – and you know I've said it before – is that if you don't fuck your husband, he will more than likely pay someone else to do the job.

And there will always be the sex industry. *Always.*

CHAPTER 3

SAMANTHA

Meeting Mr Big

He annoyed me from the second he made contact with me.

> *Dear Samantha. Wonderful profile and even more*
> *wonderful, you are touring Melbourne. I would like*
> *to make a two-hour appointment with you. The*
> *kind of service I'm looking for is sexy GFE with a*
> *'twist' of PSE. I am late 40s, hail from New York*
> *and am an entrepreneur. Regards, The Peacock.*

It's surprising how in just a few sentences he managed to irritate me. Firstly 'twist of PSE' – yuck, yuck. To anyone who is not in the sex industry, GFE means girlfriend experience (kisses, cuddles and normal sex) and PSE (porn star experience) means you up the ante a bit in the bedroom with a bit of COF,* Spanish,† Tromboning,‡ CIM,§ maybe even CIMWS¶ (never my thing) – and for the really adventurous, Greek** (gives me haemorrhoids just thinking about it). Most escorts charge extra for these services.

I don't mind some acronym fun in the bedroom, but there are some sex acts I draw the line at. Golden showers: tried it – I get stage fright and I don't like the smell of wee. Pain – but I've not met one client who wants that, apart from the odd slap on my bum. Instead, I've found that clients refuse to even pull my hair when I ask.

'Sorry, Samantha, I just don't feel right about hurting you,' whispered a very nervous bank teller as he gently tugged a strand of my hair like he was carefully handling a baby bird.

And, of course, anal. Anyone who has read my first book knows that no one goes near my bottom, but there was this client who I called 'the mushroom man': a Chinese supermarket owner with a penis the size of a curled-up

---

* COF: Cum on face.
† Spanish: Penis between boobs.
‡ Tromboning: Involves bottoms and a hand job.
§ CIM: Cum in mouth.
¶ CIMWS: Same but with swallow.
** Greek: Anal.

button mushroom, who pleaded with me to let him prod his little fungus into my bum for an extra $500. I knew I wouldn't feel a thing so I said yes. And I was right: I've had way more painful (and exciting) bowel movements.

Back to this PSE: to be honest, most men I've come across have no idea what PSE is and find the whole porn-star thing a bit intimidating. I even had a client complain to me after our date because he found the sex with me 'too forward' and 'too raunchy' for his liking.

'Samantha, please can you be gentle and loving next time?' he said over the phone the next day, shyly trying not to offend me.

'I am terribly sorry, Brett, I probably got carried away,' I replied, half mortified and half amused. If only the public knew what this industry was really like!

But a *twist* of PSE – what the hell did that mean? It meant he was annoying, that's what. He'd probably use other phrases that grate on me, like, 'Let's hook up and GRAB a coffee', or 'Let's TOUCH BASE next week', or 'I'll REACH OUT to you tomorrow'.

Another thing: what kind of person labels themselves an entrepreneur? Was he too dumb to be hired and/or always getting fired, so he called himself as entrepreneur? Boss of his own sad little world? Couldn't he have been more specific?

Lastly, let's not overlook the most irritating part of his email: his signature. Who the fuck calls themselves 'The Peacock'? For a start, he was clearly a regular on the escort scene: he had fired off his email to me the second my tour dates to Melbourne were posted online, which smacked of ickiness. He knew the terminology, plus I'm sure he had invented his (ridiculous) name years ago. But why Peacock? He either had a cock the size of a little green pea and/or he strutted around like a show-off peacock. (I would find out that the latter was true – he was certainly not small in the trouser department).

I wrote back: *No problem, sounds good, love to see you. How does 7.30 p.m. sound on Tuesday evening? I arrive at 5 p.m.* Keep it simple, no need to say much more than that. The last thing I wanted was to indulge in an email conversation with a man who called himself The Peacock.

Perhaps I was being a bit harsh. There were two things I did like about him: he came from New York and lived in Melbourne. I love American men, and anyone who knows me well knows how much I love Melbourne.

Melbourne is my favourite city in Australia. (Mind you, I went to Perth recently – such a lovely place, like Melbourne-by-the-sea. The men are so well dressed, too – like the men in Melbourne.) Yep, I could live in Melbourne if it weren't for that blanket of greyness and the fact you still wear your black winter clothes in the summer. But, being a Londoner, I can relate to the storm clouds. Then there are the great restaurants; the winter fashion; the buzz of the bustling bars. The terrible traffic; the elegant shops at the Paris end of Collins Street; that wonderfully expensive shoe boutique Miss Louise, nestled next to the Westin Hotel, where I bought a pair of red Valentino shoes for $800 and slipped them on the second I handed over the cash. I couldn't tell you how many Melbournites stopped me that day to tell me how much they loved my shoes. No surprise, of course – they recognise style when they see it! Even when I was resting on a bench rubbing my blistered feet, the compliments were still coming.

Of course – and far more important than red shoes – I love the handsome, sophisticated, slick men. I've travelled the world, I've been to a lot of countries and cities – and I stand by my words that men from Melbourne are the best looking in the world. What this city lacks in weather it certainly makes up for in gorgeousness when walking through the CBD: a sea of handcrafted European suits, expensive colourful ties, leather Italian shoes. Even the tradies in their neon jackets, drilling holes in the pavement, are hot.

From the second I boarded my first-ever Qantas flight to Melbourne and did a quick scan of my fellow passengers, from elegant women with smart scarves around their necks to handsome well-dressed businessmen with good hair – jolly good – the old British snob in me was well and truly still there. I felt like I was home: there wasn't a hoodie or thong in sight.

That flight was for my first 'tour' as Samantha. What's a tour? It's when you can make a lot of money quickly. Escorts announce their tour dates on social media and cram in as many or as few clients as they like while visiting different cities. It's a good way to build clientele, make a lot of money and travel. I once made $20 000 cash in five days in Perth. (And anyone who gasps at me revealing that fact – yes, I put it in the bank and paid my taxes. If any burglars are reading this: don't bother robbing my house – there's no big box of cash under my bed. The only thing you'll find is the stinky pillow my Jack Russell, Georgie, sleeps on and a bunch of lolly wrappers that my daughter shoves down the side of the bed when she sleeps with me.)

I often play spot-the-hooker on planes, airports and hotels – and, as the cliché goes, it's always the well-dressed woman. (Except for me right now, on a flight to Melbourne wearing Jesus sandals, tracksuit bottoms, zero make-up, a white singlet with a hole in it and half my fake eyelashes missing. If any other escorts were on this plane playing spot-the-hooker, they would either look at me pityingly or, worse, not even notice me at all.)

Another thing I fell in love with in Melbourne was my hotel: a cool, arty, funky place nestled in an expensive suburb next to the boutique shops and great restaurants. The minute I glided through the lobby doors and was greeted by friendly, bright young faces and the smell of tuberose and sandalwood, I knew this was the place for me. Whether they knew what I did and didn't care, or didn't know and didn't care anyway, the team there made me truly feel at home. Nothing was ever too much trouble, not even when some 19-year-old student client started stalking me and they moved me quickly and efficiently and without any questions to another suite and promptly changed my reservation to a 'silent' booking – which means that every time I stay, if someone calls up asking for me they say, 'I'm sorry, sir, we have no one here with that name.' It's a good thing to know about as I've heard from plenty of escorts that disgruntled clients who know your real name will threaten to call hotel reception to tell them about 'a PROSTITUTE IN ROOM 107!!!' which will usually send the poor women into a panic. But if they don't know you're there, you're not there: 'I'm sorry sir, we have no PROSTITUTE by that name here ...' (And no doubt the young men on the Concierge desk spend their lunch hour googling said PROSTITUTE ... and probably wish they got paid enough money to nip up there for a quickie.)

So: back to Big. The Peacock. I'm not going to give too much away just yet, but I will tell you this:

1) He was gorgeous.
2) He smelled nice.
3) He had a great cock.
4) He fucked well.
5) And he was nice to talk to.

To look at, he was my type 100 per cent. His eyes were green (or blue, depending on which light he looked at you in), his hair sandy and lots of it, and his arms – the make-or-break for me – were straining under his navy Zegna suit. And his name ... as I carefully took his jacket off to hang it up, I saw sewn into it an expensive-looking label. I smiled: he even had a nice name.

Come on – names are important too. They are! I once dated someone called Brian. I knew he wasn't going to be my husband purely based on his name. Another ex had an awful surname: Grunty. No chance of me daydreaming about our wedding ... or being Mrs Grunty. So seeing that Mr Big had a nice, solid name, I felt a little bit more attracted to him. But for the sake of protecting his identity, I decided to steal the masked identity of Carrie Bradshaw's Mr Big in *Sex and the City*. Because, really, my Mr Big was just like that Mr Big: tall, handsome, a New Yorker, sophisticated, ever-so-slightly intimidating. Okay, I knew he really was just a normal boring businessman but he had something I liked. I couldn't put my finger on it. It was chemistry, I think. *A feeling.*

As soon as he answered the door and I saw a tall, well-dressed man with sexy eyes and a genuine smile that lit up his face, I froze momentarily.

Shit. I hadn't been expecting that.

I wasn't often lost for words. I could fill the most awkward of silences.

'Can I get you something, a Champagne perhaps?'

'Um, a drink would be nice!' I smiled nervously, popping my bag down on the carpet. 'I'll have whatever you're having.'

'Sure, Champagne for the lady,' he said in a soft American accent, smiling, opening the fridge. 'I must say, Samantha, it really is lovely to finally meet you. You are more beautiful in the flesh, I might add.'

I smiled as he poured me a glass.

Well, well, well. So this was The Peacock. The Entrepreneur. GFE with a 'twist' of PSE. The man behind that irritating email was actually quite nice.

Sometimes I do get it wrong, I thought as I glanced at his expensive watch and silver cufflinks, his graceful hands and manicured nails. Thank goodness I had agreed to see him. To think I had almost said no to meeting this one, The Peacock! *Should I ask him why he calls himself that*, I wondered, finding myself glancing at his groin. *Next time*, I thought, doing a double-take. Jesus, was it really that big? It certainly looked a bit packed in there ... Hopefully there would be a next time.

Mr Big, while friendly, wasn't much of a talker. He didn't give me any information about his private life, really, except that he was from Staten Island originally and had been living in Melbourne for ten years; he had a business that I didn't really understand, had two kids and had separated from his wife long ago. That's all I got out of him in two hours. And that was fine by me. He wasn't a client who wanted to talk a lot: he wanted to release tension. I had no problem with that.

He had a lovely, big, throbbing cock that he eased into my pussy with such skill he made me orgasm at least twice in two hours (and I didn't need to fake them). When he came he looked in my eyes and smiled, then nuzzled his head into my neck lovingly.

'Samantha, thank you,' he said, stroking my hair as we cuddled.

This was a man who loved women – or, at least, paying for women. *What is he paying for?* I pondered as he finally threw himself back on the bed, panting. Was he paying for the ease? The fact that there are no games? That when you hand me $2000 in cash for two hours in a hotel room, you are most definitely going to get sex without the pain-in-the-arse game-playing before, during and after? Because this man would have no problem meeting women; they would probably throw themselves at him. He was handsome, charming, with a sexy accent, and he was easy company. And his cock: well ...!

'Thank you, Samantha,' he said again after a few minutes had passed. 'I had such a lovely time. But, sadly, work beckons ...' And with that Big gave me a quick kiss on the lips before untangling himself from the sheets.

'I can stay if you like!' I wanted to plead. Instead the words, 'No problem!' came out, and I hoped the disappointment wasn't written all over my face. The time had gone so quickly, my usual trick of counting down the minutes forgotten. I didn't want it to end. I liked this man. I liked his smell, I liked his body, I liked his cock. I liked this *feeling*.

I watched as he pulled his shirt on, carefully doing up button by button as he looked at his reflection in the mirror. There was no small talk, no awkward conversation about what I was doing for the rest of the day, and did I like Australia, and where in London I was from. Big felt comfortable enough – or didn't care enough – to fill the silence.

I wasn't feeling as relaxed, though. Awkwardly I put my dress back on and brushed my hair, feeling nervous and speculating about him. Where was he going – back to the office to shout at a few people? Where did any of my clients go afterwards? Back home, where their wives were waiting with dinner in the oven, blissfully ignorant that their husbands had just had their cocks in my mouth?

Big was probably going somewhere exciting – some cool bar, or an expensive restaurant for a business meeting with more well-dressed, powerful men. Maybe he even had a date with a beautiful woman.

I would have done anything to be able to go with him, to hang off his arm and laugh at his jokes and clink our Champagne glasses together.

As I stared at him, it was pretty bloody obvious to me that something was happening. Something I had been warned about by Nina, my very first madam, and by the Russian boss of an escort agency who told me once in his broken English: *Never fall in love with a client. It always ends in heartbreak. It never works. The girl always gets hurt.*

'The man never, ever lets the girl forget where he met her,' Nina said sharply once. I had scoffed at the idea: fall in love with a client? Were they joking? Half the time I couldn't wait for the clients to bloody leave the room.

But here, with Big, it was different. *He* was different. Was he going to be *that* client?

I was worried the answer was going to be yes. I thought I was going to fall in love with Big. And that wasn't good news. That wasn't good news at all.

Especially because I didn't know if I'd ever see him again.

CHAPTER 4

SAMANTHA

The importance of a good review

Every escort has at least one or two regular clients; they are our bread and butter. When the phone is quiet and there's no money coming in – usually during school holidays (clients are with their families) and tax time (they're poor) – you can always count on your regulars to still want to see you. They will move mountains to see you and, equally, the escort will move mountains to see them. They take priority over new clients and, quite often, over our social lives too. You don't piss off a regular. There are a thousand other escorts he can choose from and, while he may like you a lot, he does hold quite a bit of (unintentional) power over you.

One of my regulars is a lawyer called Mark. He is fifty-two, comes from London originally and dresses sharply: he's the type who can carry off a pink tie and a matching handkerchief, and glasses with a bright neon frame. He has a massive head of thick greying hair that would make every balding man jealous. So much so that after a few drinks I always tease him and call him Microphone Head.

'Testing, testing!' I giggle, patting the top of his fluffy hair. He doesn't mind – or he pretends not to, at least.

We share a fair bit in common – we are both London snobs and readily admit it; we have a very British sense of self-deprecating humour and it's actually quite comforting to talk to someone from your home town about *EastEnders* or how in Australia Christmas never feels like Christmas. Brits just get it.

Mark speaks like an actor in *Downton Abbey* and is one of the kindest men I know. Still, his wife decided that she didn't love him anymore after twenty-three years of marriage and I helped him build his confidence back. We have been seeing each other for a few years and I am very, very fond of him.

He writes me beautiful cards with lovely, carefully-thought-out words about how special I am in his life, and he is always the first to call to see if I am okay, or how my holiday was, or to say that if I ever need anything – especially legal advice – to give him a call.

'Seriously, Samantha, I mean it. I'll be really cross if you don't ask me for help,' he would say sometimes, looking at me earnestly. His kindness can be overwhelming.

Something else about Mark: he is probably my kinkiest client. While we love our intimate dinners and trips overseas, he does love a good dirty fuck. Preferably with a few people at the same time. And it took us a year of seeing each other before he felt comfortable enough to tell me, while I was sipping an espresso martini at the bar of a very well-known five-star hotel in Sydney's CBD.

'Darling, I've got an idea and I want you to do something for me – for us – tonight,' he said, beckoning me to sit closer.

'Of course! Whatever you like,' I replied, putting my glass down. I would do pretty much anything for Mark, especially on that night. We'd had a lovely afternoon; he had been so generous. We'd met at David Jones for oysters and Champagne, then Mark had insisted on taking me shopping. One Hervé Leger dress ($1000) and a pair of Stuart Weitzman thigh-high burgundy suede boots ($1500) later, we had come back to the hotel for dinner and drinks.

Mark looked at me and put down his fork. 'I want you to find another cock to fuck tonight while I watch,' he said triumphantly, his eyes twinkling from behind his neon frames.

Oh. Oh shit. Really?

I stared at him and then I stared at the hotel bar. Was this the reason for the extravagant gifts? Apart from an elderly couple playing bridge, I didn't fancy our chances of finding someone else. For fuck's sake! Couldn't he have given me some warning? Did he think I could just magic a spare obliging cock out of nowhere? It was a Tuesday night, it was raining, the bar was empty ... My tummy was bloated and full from tapas, and the last thing I wanted was to have sex with Mark, let alone someone else ...

So, of course, I did what a good escort does: I lied through my bleached teeth.

'Of course I can find someone else!' I replied brightly. 'What a wonderful idea! How sexy! You're so clever in thinking up exciting ideas, aren't you, Mark?'

'Good!' he grinned, getting up, but not before giving me a quick peck on my forehead. 'That's my girl! Always up for a challenge. That's why you're my number one lady!'

As he marched off briskly to the bathroom, I wondered how the fuck I was going to pull this one off. Samantha X was clever. She was smart. She could often do the impossible. But this? Finding another man at 9.30 p.m. on a dead Tuesday night? It wasn't just impossible – it would be a fucking miracle.

Interrupting my panicky thoughts was the barman. 'Excuse me, miss, would you like another drink?'

'What? Oh yes, um, sure. Yes, please,' I replied, glancing up briefly. 'I'll have ...'

Hang on.

Hang on a minute.

The barman? The barman! Of course! I could ask the bloody barman! I mean, he was okay-looking – a bit short, possibly Spanish, but so what? Europeans love women ... He had a cock, he was a man ... He was the only bloody decent man in this place.

I squinted at his name tag and took a deep breath.

'Look, Manuel,' I hissed, grabbing his arm. I had to get this done before Mark came back from the bathroom. 'I am an escort – an expensive one. I am with a very important client. I will pay you $500 to have sex with me in front of him. That's all you need to do. Five hundred dollars cash. No penis-on-penis. Just have sex with me and then go. Will you do it? Please? We are staying upstairs.'

I must have sounded either completely mad or completely desperate – probably both. But Manuel looked at me with only one thing in his eyes: fear.

'Um, miss, thank you, but I cannot do this thing you ask of me,' he said nervously. 'It is my first shift here, miss, and my boss is here and I will lose my job. I am sorry, miss.'

He shuffled away and cowered behind the bar, not daring to even look in my direction.

'So how did you go?' Mark asked, pulling his chair up again. 'Any luck?'

'No, not yet, darling, but let me work on it,' I said, feeling worried now. I couldn't let Mark down. I just couldn't.

'Just give me some time,' I pleaded. 'Can you go for a walk or something? I just feel more confident asking a man when you're not around ... I don't want to scare them off. Sorry, darling, is that okay?'

And Mark, being the sweet man he is, picked up his phone, and off he went.

'I'll be back in ten minutes,' he said, 'for our threesome!'

I smiled weakly. Jesus Christ. How was this my life now? The most exciting group activity I usually got up to was dinner with my mum friends and our kids. And here I was trying to find more cock for my 'eager' pussy. It would be hilarious if this wasn't actually happening to me.

I scanned the room. There were a few couples – no. The pensioners playing bridge – no, thanks, and besides, our room didn't have wheelchair access.

What looked like drinks between business colleagues – no, and how awkward would that be?

Then there was the useless bloody barman, who was scared of his boss.

His boss.

Who the hell was his boss?

'Is everything okay, madam?' A velvety Irish accent interrupted my thinking. I looked up. A handsome young man with a neat beard and dark hair was looking at me, smiling. He was smartly dressed in a grey suit and white shirt, with his name displaying his name and title: *Rohan Fitzgerald, Hotel Bar Manager.*

I'd found the boss. Or, rather, the boss had found me.

'Rohan, good evening,' I purred in my sexiest Samantha voice, uncrossing and crossing my legs, showing a glimpse of my lingerie. 'I have a very strange but wonderful question for you. Would you like to hear it?'

'Try me,' he said, smiling.

'I am a very expensive escort,' I said slowly and in my poshest London accent. 'I am here with my very wealthy client who wants to pay you five hundred dollars to fuck me in front of him. My client is straight – he just wants to watch.'

Here we go … We'll probably get chucked out of this hotel now. How embarrassing …

'Sure, why not?' he replied as if I'd just asked him for a lemonade. 'Do I get the cash upfront?'

I blinked. Did I hear that right?

'You will?' I stammered. 'You will have sex with me?'

'Yeah, but do I get the cash upfront?'

'Yes! Yes, you'll get the cash upfront! Room 101. Fifteen minutes!'

I squealed with excitement when Mark came back. 'I've found one! Rohan, the bar manager! Hurry up! He'll be up in fifteen ... oh and we have to give him five hundred upfront ... He wants the money upfront!'

Mark grinned at me. 'I knew you wouldn't let me down, Samantha,' he said, pressing the button for the lift. 'You never do.'

I smiled weakly. Bloody hell – this was really happening. I'd never done this before, but as in all my bookings, I had to take charge. The men were relying on my professionalism to make it smooth sailing and natural. And you know the saying: fake it until you make it. Don't let anyone suspect for one second that you are a complete and utter fraud. (That goes for every profession, by the way.)

True to his word, fifteen minutes later Rohan the bar manager was tapping on our door.

'Hi, come in, come in,' I said, grateful that Rohan had even turned up. 'Mark's in the shower. He's really nice, don't be nervous.' I smiled briefly. Could he tell I was the nervous one?

Rohan, on the other hand, looked as cool as a bloody cucumber, like he did this every night of the week. *Fuck a hooker and her client – what, AGAIN?* That's what he was probably thinking. *Can't I just have a quiet night off for once?*

'So this is what you do, then?' Rohan said, eyeing all my expensive shopping bags as he took off his tie.

'Er, yes,' I replied, slightly embarrassed, dismissing the bags with my hand. What was he thinking? Was I being quietly judged? I looked down, not wanting to meet his eyes. This whole bloody situation was embarrassing. Sex with strangers for money I can do; sex with a hot young man who is not paying me is different.

'And how much do you get paid?'

'Um, oooh, around five thousand dollars?'

'Five thousand a month?'

'Um, ha! I mean, no … five thousand for the night.'

'Jesus Christ Mother Mary, I'm in the wrong fucking job,' he said, whistling.

'Oh well, not too late to make the change.' I smiled, counting out five green notes from the white envelope Mark had given me and handing them to him.

Just then Mark padded out of the bathroom wearing nothing but a fluffy white bathrobe.

'Ah good, Samantha, you've paid Rohan,' he said, plonking himself on a chair next to the bed. 'Rohan, she's a very good girl, isn't she? I am sure you will love your time with her.'

Rohan and I locked eyes and grinned at each other. Rohan was handsome. And young – twenty-four at most. With a great body. I had to admit I was pretty lucky. Most of my clients, although lovely and kind, were the wrong side of fifty with droopy bums and grey pubes. It wasn't often I got to run my hands over a toned, taut and tanned young body. It was pretty hard not to laugh out loud at my luck, actually. If only the school mums could see me now!

'Right, well, you're gonna have to tell me what to do here,' Rohan said.

Okay, Samantha, here we go. Put on your best front. This is showtime.

'Let's start with this,' I purred, unzipping his flies with a condom in my mouth as he shut his eyes and arched back.

The sex wasn't outrageous, but I enjoyed every sweet, short moment. Rohan was lying on top of me, his cock plunging in and out while he kept his brown eyes on mine.

'Like this?' he whispered, obviously determined to do a good job.

'Perfect,' I mouthed back, spreading my legs wider. 'Just take my lead …'

'Mark,' I said more loudly, 'are you watching Rohan's hard cock fucking my wet pussy, darling? See how hard and thick it is? See how wet I am?'

Mark was utterly transfixed; one hand on his cock, which was standing so upright it was prodding his belly button.

'Oh yes,' he murmured, in a trance. 'Lovely.' His eyes were firmly on my pussy being pounded. The harder Rohan fucked me, the harder Mark's cock looked to be. 'Rohan, how does her pussy feel?'

'Gorgeous,' Rohan replied in his rich Irish accent. 'She feels tight, so tight.'

Then suddenly, a loud groan. Mark had blown all over his dressing gown and all over his abdomen. Rohan and I both glanced over. There was an awful lot of cum.

Mark was still groaning when Rohan whispered in my ear, 'Samantha, may I please ejaculate now?'

'Yes.'

'And where I am allowed to ejaculate please?'

I glanced at Mark, who was still in post-orgasmic bliss.

'Um, on my tits? I don't know, really. Wherever you …'

'Fuck,' he moaned, whipping off the condom and blowing all over my stomach before I could finish my sentence. For a few seconds, there was silence. All I could hear was the beating of our hearts, mine slightly faster than his – probably because it was more than twenty years older than his and not as fit. Then Rohan's voice jolted me.

'Right, thanks for that,' he said, peeling himself off me. 'I'd better get back to work.'

He started getting ready quickly, and before I could get up he was dressed and ready to go, patting his trouser pocket as if to make sure his cash was there. He wasn't cold so much as efficient.

'Oh no, thank *you*,' I replied, pulling the sheets over my naked breasts.

I won't lie: it was a bit awkward. For Mark and me anyway. While we felt comfortable with each other – remember, we'd known each other for years – now, in a hotel room with this confident young man who we had just paid to have sex with me … This was a time when we bonded in our typically British awkwardness. We looked at each other, and for once I was lost for words.

'Um, yes, well, thank you, Rohan, it was jolly nice of you to oblige,' stammered Mark, holding out his hand, then quickly putting it down again when he saw Rohan raise an eyebrow and edge away.

'Yeah, no worries,' Rohan said and headed towards the door. I could sense the relief in Mark as he went to turn the door handle.

'Oh, before I go, can I ask you guys a favour?' Rohan asked earnestly, turning round to look at us.

'Of course!' Mark and I replied in unison, probably a little bit too brightly.

'Can you write a good review of me on TripAdvisor?'

Mark and I looked at each other. Did we really just hear that? Fucking *TripAdvisor*?

'Of course we can!' we chimed in unison, again in our British nothing-is-ever-too-much-trouble way.

'Cheers, guys,' Rohan said with a grin, giving us the thumbs-up. The door slammed behind him, leaving me and Mark in silence, staring at each other, before we burst out laughing. Bloody TripAdvisor?

And because Mark and I were decent folk who kept our word, Rohan the bar manager got five stars for his wonderful service, top-class professionalism and second-to-none warm and very intimate customer service.

CHAPTER 5

SAMANTHA
(BUT REALLY AMANDA)

Falling for Big

So it happened. Everything I had been warned about – all the hurt and pain of dating a client – went out the window and I fell head over heels in love with Mr Big.

And I realised I was in love with him one night in Sydney, over tuna sashimi in a fancy Japanese restaurant, four months after we'd first met.

'... And so in a nutshell that's why we split,' he said in his soft American accent in between mouthfuls of brown rice. But I wasn't listening: I was just staring at his thick, tanned fingers holding the porcelain chopsticks, the glint of his Tag white-gold watch in the light, and the way he sipped his sake and licked his lips after.

He looked so handsome in his navy shirt and blue denim jeans, and I could smell his expensive aftershave, just slightly, enough to ignite a feeling inside me, a swirling, whirling feeling of desire. *That feeling.*

Was it normal to fall in love with a client? Did other escorts do the same?

I had met a lot of men in my job. Hundreds. I dreaded to think how many condoms I'd slipped on with my mouth, how many orgasms I'd had – real ones and fake; how many hotel rooms I'd seen, how many sad stories I'd heard, how many white envelopes I'd slipped into my bag, how many hotel lobbies I'd glided through. But it didn't matter, because it all blended into one big blur.

Since meeting Big, I couldn't really think of anyone else. Sure, I still saw clients, but there was only one thing on my mind when I was with them: Big.

Since the first time we'd met in my hotel room in Melbourne, we had seen each other regularly and become extremely close. We'd sneak in quick weekday lunches followed by a kiss in his car, or a coffee date when he was pushed for time, just so he could see how I'd been. He would always slide over a gift: a box from Georg Jensen or Tiffany.

'Just something small,' he'd say with a smile. Small – like a diamond. How could I *not* fall in love with this man?

'I care for you, Samantha,' he told me once as we sat huddled together in one of his favourite Italian cafes in Melbourne's Lygon Street, having coffee with biscotti. 'I know I shouldn't cross that boundary, but I do, I really do.'

I'd had such a good time in Melbourne, mostly due to meeting him, that I was visiting a few times a month, when the kids were with their dad for the week. Most of my clients I'd met that first trip booked me again – including Big, who tended to book early mornings on his way to work. It was a lovely way to start the day.

The sex kept getting better and better. I was beginning to feel comfortable with him. I never wanted our time to end.

'Can I order up a coffee for you?' I'd always ask just as our time was nearing its close, not because I wanted a coffee but because he would often say 'yes' and I knew (a) the coffee would take ages to come and (b) that meant I could spend longer in his arms.

So when he told me he was coming to Sydney for business and asked if I wanted to have a dinner date with him, I could barely contain my excitement. Our first proper dinner date! A night-time date! For once, I could be with him in public! I could hang off his arm! Pretend to be his girlfriend!

'I would love to!' I had replied as calmly as I could, and as I hung up the phone I did a little dance around my bedroom. *Big's coming to Sydney! Big's coming to Sydney!* What should I wear? I'd have to have my hair blow-dried, naturally. And my nails – red or nude?

For the dinner I chose a low-cut black lace dress and my knee-high black suede boots – no panties – and decided red over nude nails. It wasn't often that I felt daring enough to wear colour on my nails but Big liked a bit of glamour; it was the New York in him. He liked me to wear make-up and to dress up, and I wanted to please him.

Most escorts offer dinner dates, typically two hours at the restaurant and two hours of 'dessert' back at the hotel. While I was $1100 for an hour, I felt $3300 for four hours was fair, so that was my rate. Dinners were at the latest, trendiest fine-dining restaurants. But 'eating' dates were troublesome. Bloating, gas, garlic breath – and that's just me. The last thing I wanted to do after a big meal and a bottle of wine was get naked with a stranger. And the more experienced an escort I became, the more confident I grew in stating my boundaries. I knew that two hours of eating would result in a bloated tummy and zero sexual desire, so I told all my regulars that instead of sex after dinner, it had to be before our meal, when I had a flat tummy and there was no chance of me feeling sleepy and falling asleep – or, worse, farting.

But I didn't need to tell Big this, purely because nothing would have killed my desire for his cock. Not even the biggest plate of pasta or entree, main course and pudding. I loved his cock; I loved our sex. I was beginning to feel more comfortable with him and more myself. Usually, with clients, I feigned confidence and made all the right noises ('Ooh, ahh, that feels amazing'), but with Big? It was different. I was more natural. More Amanda than Samantha. And as an escort, you need to tread a fine line. Show glimmers of who you are, but not give them too much.

Lots of escorts I know have partners and kids. Their clients are rarely aware of this. 'I don't want to bring my private life into the booking,' one told me once. 'The clients don't need to know. They like to think they're in with a chance.'

She was right, of course. Yet Big felt like more than just a client to me. He was someone I would date in my real life. He was someone Amanda would be attracted to – and Amanda was really fussy.

'Samantha, I like you. I really like you,' Big said quietly, holding my hand under the table as the waitress cleared the plates away. 'I've seen a few escorts in my time, but you? You're different. You have something I haven't found in a woman before. You're classy, funny, intelligent. You're beautiful ...'

And as I was staring into his eyes, trying to dive into them, he pulled out a small navy box.

'I hope you don't mind, but I bought you a gift, just something small,' he smiled, passing it to me.

Carefully I opened the box and pick up the sparkling silver chain with a small diamond encrusted in the centre.

'Oh my god, Big, it's beautiful!' No one had bought me a gift like this before!

'It's white gold,' he said, his voice warm as he slipped it around my neck. 'And the diamond sparkles in the light, just like you. Meeting you was the best thing that's happened to me in a long while, Samantha. Wear it and think of me, your Melbourne man who ... who likes you a lot.'

Then he kissed me on my lips, right there in the middle of a bustling restaurant with its nosy diners who turned their heads to catch a glimpse of the handsome man and the woman he was kissing, right there! 'It's me!' I wanted to shriek. 'The handsome man is kissing *me*!'

'Let's go,' I whispered, feeling the desire sweep up from my toes to my head.

I didn't want to go back to a soulless hotel room and make love on a bland, uncomfortable hotel bed. I was sick to death of hotels. The lack of personality in a hotel was perfect for a nameless client, but not for him. I knew it wasn't wise letting a client into my home – I'd never done it before, so I knew I shouldn't, even though we'd been seeing each other for six months. But I knew he wasn't weird or a serial killer or a mad rapist. He was smart, successful, wealthy and kind.

I wanted him in my home.

I wanted him in my bed, with my mess and my battered Nike runners in the hallway; with my photos of my late grandfather and great aunt Violet.

I daydreamed about doing nice, normal things with Big like watching a movie or discussing our day over a nice glass of red, as he was cutting up herbs for our stir fry (I'm a terrible cook).

I wanted him in my *life*.

I could list all the reasons why he should have come back to mine and I could list a million reasons why he shouldn't. But that's a conversation for another day. Because he didn't.

Less than twenty minutes later we were tangled on his hotel sheets, panting and gasping.

'Oh, Big,' I breathed, 'I love the way you touch me ...'

'Samantha,' he panted back, 'you drive me wild. I've never wanted a woman so much.'

And for the first time in a long time, I didn't just have sex with a client: I made love to the man I was in love with. And wow – it had been a long time since I'd felt that.

'It's been four hours,' I panted, glancing at my watch, momentarily pulling myself away from him. 'I should go.'

'You're not going anywhere,' he said, pulling me on top of him again, opening my legs up and forcing his cock into me.

I'd love to say we slept in each other's arms all night, but we hardly slept – Big wouldn't let me and I didn't want to waste time closing my eyes when I had my delicious Mr Big from Melbourne who smelled nice in bed with me all night. The next morning, he left before I woke. There was an envelope with $3300 cash in it and a note in his scribbly but perfect writing. Even his handwriting turned me on.

'Samantha, you sleep like an angel. Sorry I had to leave – work meeting. Apologies, I'm a bit short on cash – wasn't expecting to stay over. Dinner again tonight? I've changed my flights.'

I smiled and threw myself back onto the pillow, pressing the envelope to my nose. Even that smelled of him.

He texted an hour later to say how nice an evening it had been.

I can't believe you gave me extra time, Samantha. You must really like me!

Amanda, I typed back. *Call me Amanda.*

And that, dear reader, is how it happens. That is how an escort falls in love with a client.

CHAPTER 6

SAMANTHA

The hermit and other strange animals

I have a client called J. There is nothing amazing about J. He is not rich, he is not handsome and he is not exciting. If there was a male equivalent to Eleanor Rigby, it would be him.

J is fifty-eight and unashamedly admits he is a recluse. His skin is waxy pale yet unblemished, and his body is not fit. Angry-looking varicose veins strain out of his calves and his swollen belly is full of processed food, but no alcohol, as lemonade is his drink of choice. He has been in the same job for twenty-two years and he sits at the same desk. He lives alone and has done most of his life. In fact, he wouldn't have it any other way. He has never had a girlfriend, although he came close to kissing a woman when he was twenty-three. He had one friend many years ago, but he died in a fiery car crash. He spends birthdays and Christmas alone, very happily. At most he will Skype his relatives in Tasmania.

'I just don't like people, Samantha,' he told me once. 'I get nervous around them.'

But I like J. I really do. He absolutely fascinates me. He is one of those clients who I could listen to for hours, and I do. I don't hear about wild adventures or how many countries he has travelled to, or how many cars he has, because he hasn't been anywhere or done anything, and he prefers the bus. In fact, apart from spending time with sex workers, I don't think he has ever done anything particularly exciting in his life.

Yet his conversation is absolutely fascinating to me purely because it is so simple, so easy. There is no kinky sex, no dirty talk. We barely even touch, except for the ten minutes in our three-hour bookings when he parts my legs gently with his trembling hand and licks my pussy like an obedient little kitten licking a saucer of milk. I cum quickly and quietly, and then we cuddle and chat for the rest of our time together. I tried to have sex with him the first time I met him and was quickly told to stop.

'I'm not very good at sex and I would rather not, thanks, Sam,' he said shyly, slowly moving my hands away. Once I knew that J just wanted company and a cuddle, I could relax and so could he.

J's life is very simple. In fact, it is beautifully simple. I meet a lot of powerful, successful men and I am always interested in hearing about their lives. But J is far more fascinating. He doesn't believe in stress. Even when there are problems at work his solution is simple: 'I just think, *Oh dear*, and go and make myself a cup of tea,' he told me. 'That usually does the trick.'

Even when his elderly mother died and he had to jump on a plane to Hobart, he showed little emotion.

Thank you, Samantha. Death is a merely a part of life, were his neat little words after I texted my condolences.

Even J's diet is simple. For breakfast, just a coffee. For lunch, a ham or beef sandwich (on white, no butter) at work, depending on whether there is mustard involved and which brand of mustard. He doesn't like Hot English because it tickles his nose and makes him sneeze, but he's rather partial to the seeded variety, as long as they don't put on too much. And then dinner. Well, dinner is the meal J looks forward to the most: a Michelle Bridges frozen meal that he heats up in the microwave. Every single evening.

'*Every* evening?' I asked him once incredulously while wiping the last few drops of his cum from his stomach with a tissue, before popping it in the bin.

'Every evening, Samantha,' he repeated seriously. 'Even Christmas. The portions are *extremely* generous.'

'And which flavour is your favourite?'

'Oooh, well ...' He whistled and then paused. He was clearly giving this some serious thought. 'I'd have to say I'm rather partial to the Italian Style Chicken. It's not too spicy and has just the right amount of flavour.'

I smiled – but J hadn't finished.

'Followed closely by the Mild Massaman Beef Curry and then the Chicken Pesto Pasta,' he continued. 'But the Salmon Fish Cakes? No, Samantha, not for me. I always find fish a bit fishy. I am just not a fish man.' He shook his head as if he had just confessed to being a war criminal for the Nazis. It was hard not to be charmed by his sweet sincerity.

J is a lovely man. He calls me 'my goddess', and I always smile when he walks into my hotel room wearing his anorak if it is raining – or even if it isn't – and his sensible clumpy shoes.

'Sorry I'm a bit late today, my goddess,' he said once, shaking the rainwater off his umbrella. 'This weather made the bus run almost eleven minutes late.'

'Don't be silly, J, it's always lovely to see you,' I replied, hanging up his dripping jacket and clicking on the kettle. And I meant it. I think I am J's only 'friend' and that is fine with me.

Escorts always have clients like J and we love them. I know I do. Why? Because they are *easy*. They're like animals – they have pure souls and pure hearts. They are kind and gentle, and treat us with the utmost respect. We don't care that they aren't handsome and exciting and rich. Give me kind, simple J over a coked-up banker any day of the week.

My rule is that the better-looking the client, the more of a pain in the arse he is. More entitled and terribly arrogant. 'You should be paying *me*!' a tall, dark young client smirked at me once as he thumbed the green hundred-dollar bills in front of me. It wasn't the first time a good-looking client had said this to me – it was almost like they were justifying why they were paying for sex.

It's hard to smile sweetly through gritted teeth when really you want to tell them you would rather poke your eyes out with hot toothpicks then spend a minute more in their company. 'AND I FAKED THEM ALL!' I have been tempted to scream to wipe the smug smiles off their faces. Instead, I say, 'Wow I *am* a lucky girl, aren't I? I really hope we can see each other again.' Then I give them the finger behind their backs as soon as they turn round to leave.

People always marvel at how escorts can have sex with ugly men. It always makes me smile, their lack of enlightenment; their shallowness. Ugly? What's ugly to you might not be ugly to me. Ugly is an unkind heart, not an unconventional face. Ugly is someone who laughs at the expense of others and shows little compassion. Ugly is arrogance, rudeness and a lack of respect. Ugly is nastiness and spite.

So how can I have sex with ugly men? The answer is, quite simply, that I don't. If someone gives away a glimmer of rudeness or arrogance over the phone or email when trying to secure a booking, I won't see him. I don't care who he is, how rich or famous he is or how big his dick is. I don't care whether he sends me selfies of his perfect abs or flexing his arms in the mirror of his gym, or whether he offers to pay triple my fee. Mental health will always, *always*, be more important to me than dollars. Even with – actually, especially with – the clients who book my Angels. I have two rules that I stick to as madam to my girls: if I wouldn't see a man – and I am fussy – then I don't let my girls see him; and if he shows a hint of rudeness or disrespect when making an appointment, I show him the proverbial door.

One engineer, who used his real work email address, was brash and aloof when trying to lock in a date with one of my Angels. *Yes/no? Am I missing something?* he wrote when I explained, for the third time, that he had to give me a few basic details about himself before I book in my girls.

Yes, I wrote back, angry now. *You are missing basic manners. You are not the kind of client I want my girls to see, sorry. There are plenty of other agencies around, I suggest you contact them.*

Thank god I have no one to answer to, no greedy pimp or emotionless female boss. It's just Vanessa and me, and we're on the same page. So what if we lost a booking? When we say we want to empower women, not exploit them, we bloody mean it.

Meet Gregory, who is just twenty-one. He is an electrician; another client whose sweetness and sincerity sticks in my mind. He has a handsome face, in a nerdy way, and wears glasses. When I met him I told him he looked like a young Clark Kent, and he does.

'Yes, guilty! It's been said before,' he admitted shyly, his eyes firmly planted on the carpet.

He had booked me for four hours at a $1800-a-night suite at the Crown Casino in Melbourne.

'Gregory! How can you afford this?' I gasped as I looked around; he was already paying me over $3000 for my time.

There was a bottle of Champagne on ice, cosy soft slippers at the end of each side of the king-size bed, and two massive bathrooms, one with a spa. And he looked so smart, too: a light grey jacket from Calibre, brown loafers from Gucci and a pale blue shirt from Armani.

'I don't have anything else to spend my money on,' he said quietly. Then, suddenly: 'Hey! Do you like the cricket?' and before I could answer he clicked on the TV.

'Yes, sure!' I lied, trying to work him out. But there was really nothing to work out. His needs were, again, very simple: he just wanted me to sit there. If I nudged closer to him, he would move away. At one stage he turned around and said seriously, 'Sorry, Samantha, but you are in my personal space.'

'Oh, sorry, am I?' I said, mortified that I had made him feel uncomfortable, and I edged even further away.

After about an hour of my eyes glazing over thanks to the cricket, and having drunk most of the Champagne as Gregory didn't drink, I decided it must be time he wanted sex. Surely he wanted sex! He was a horny 21-year-old! The thing was, I couldn't even sit close to him, so how was I going to make him come to the bedroom with me?

'Why don't I take your jacket off and hang it up for you?' I asked, reaching over. 'Can I fetch one of those nice dressing gowns for you? They look so fluffy and cosy –'

'No!' he cried, inching away even more. 'Sorry, Samantha, I didn't mean to snap at you. It's just that I am really proud of my clothes. I wish I could wear clothes like this every day – like wear them in an office – but I'm an electrician, so I can't. So if it's all the same to you, I'd like to keep them on all night.'

His sweet and honest nature was humbling. The most physical we got was a kiss (no tongues) before he gently pushed me away.

'That's enough for one night, I think,' he said. It was the first time I'd been told that in a booking – was I being scolded?

'I'll get my coat?' I said and went to stand up.

'No, please stay,' he responded seriously. 'We can watch TV. *CSI* is on. Do you like *CSI*?'

'Yes, I like *CSI*,' I replied slowly, sitting down again.

So for four hours we sat and stared at the TV screen, barely talking. Gregory wasn't just comfortable in our silence – he was happy. So I kicked off my Jimmy Choos, picked up the box of chocolates on the coffee table in front of me, and put my feet up. If Gregory was happy with just being in my company, I was going sit back, relax and enjoy the evening with a sweet, shy and awkward young man who had spent an awful lot of money for me to sit here with him.

The next morning, just as I was brushing my teeth, he sent me a little text message: *Thank you, Samantha, for the best night of my life.*

I smiled as toothpaste dribbled down my chin. The lovely thing was, I think he really meant it.

CHAPTER 7

AMANDA

Italy

'So will you come?' Big asked me, stroking my face, as we lay together one morning after our favourite pastime – apart from eating Italian food: sex. 'London for a few days, then to Lake Como, to my favourite hotel. It means taking a few weeks off work. Can I tear you away from your other clients, Amanda?'

'Yes,' I interrupted myself with a kiss. 'Yes, yes, yes. Love to. Of course I'll come! Thank you. What a lovely invitation.'

Well, how about that! We'd been seeing each other for six months, and now I was going on my very first overseas trip with a client. Jetsetting to the other side of the world with a 'gentleman'. Samantha X wasn't just an escort – she was an international business-class (sometimes first-class) flying companion! How times had changed since my days working at the Bordello. How *I* had changed!

Except there was one problem.

I was completely and utterly in love with Big.

He could have said 'Jump off the bridge' and I would have eagerly agreed, even though I am scared of water. It's my London background, you see – I'm not a coward, just scared of the ocean here in Australia. Us Northerners are used to the calm waters of the Mediterranean.

I'm a city girl. Put me in the middle of a crowded subway in New York at one in the morning and no idea where I'm going and I'll be fine, plus I'll make a few friends along the way. Put me in the ocean at Bondi Beach knee deep and I will have a panic attack. Not because a great white could take me, but because little things like a minnow could accidentally brush past my leg, or a gentle wave could knock me down.

I once thought about jacking in Samantha to be a Qantas flight attendant; I went as far as looking at the requirements online. When I saw that diving and swimming were part of the test, my tummy went into knots. Forget that. The plane would land safely in the middle of the Atlantic but I would manage to drown most of the passengers who were relying on me to lead them to land.

So, to recap, my love for Big wasn't sensible. It didn't come from the head; it came from my sensitive, fragile heart. You know how the old cliché goes, about fluttering tummies when you are with the one you love? That was my tummy with him. My pussy would even pulsate too; my knickers would dampen. I felt sexual, beautiful and sensual when I was with him. Even the sound of his voice turned me on. He was a real man and he made me feel like a real woman. He loved the curves of my child-bearing hips, and my wobbly bum. He loved it when I was a few kilos heavier and told me off at times for being too skinny. He said he preferred his women to be real women, like Sophia Loren. He'd always snake his arms around my waist when we were walking. And he made me feel as though I was the most sexy and beautiful woman in the world.

'I care for you so much,' he told me once as we sat huddled together, his hands twisting in mine. 'I know I shouldn't, but I do. I can't stop thinking about you.'

And the gifts! A Montblanc pen (the Grace Kelly limited edition one), a Stella McCartney bag, clothes from Scanlan Theodore, paintings from Paris and, of course, jewellery – lots and lots of jewellery.

'I just want to add a little more elegance to an already elegant woman,' he'd say, kissing my forehead, slipping another necklace worth thousands of dollars into my hands. Julia Roberts, eat your heart out!

All my old pieces I reluctantly put away: the lovely gold necklace Tab and my best friends bought me for my fortieth; the rings I had carefully chosen in quirky boutiques in Bondi. No, no, no – they wouldn't do anymore. I was with Big now; I had to up the ante.

True, some of the clothes were not to my taste. Some of the designs made me look like an overdressed Toorak housewife suffocating in white shirts that covered me from neck to groin, and lace neck-crushing dresses that I wasn't dainty enough for. I was more a denim-shorts-and-thongs kind of girl; I lived by the beach. But Big and his Melbourne taste preferred a certain style of woman – and he had such great style that I decided to try to like the clothes he gave me.

Big also liked me wearing make-up and he was the only man I knew who preferred lash extensions on me as he said they 'make your eyes stand out'.

He would notice everything. 'Darling, we need to get you a new bag,' he said once, eyeing my tatty brown leather bag. The next week, when he picked me up at the airport, he reached to the back seat of his car and handed me a personalised leather bag worth a few thousand dollars.

'Now don't get stains on it this time,' he scolded with a smile as I opened the bag.

Every time we went shopping, he would insist on buying me an expensive gift.

'Amanda, come here.' He would beckon with his finger while we were browsing some designer shop.

'No,' I would always hiss quietly, hiding from him.

'I said come *here*,' he'd smile. 'Try these on.' Handing me some ridiculously expensive sunglasses.

'No! No, that's really sweet of you, but I'm fine really, I don't need them,' I would protest sincerely. You can call me many things but a taker I am not. I know a lot of girls would use his generosity to their advantage, dragging him around the shops, pointing out expensive dresses they had to have, or jewelled bracelets that had to be theirs. But I never asked for any of it; not a single thing. And this time, again, my words were ignored.

'She's having them,' he would say, grinning at the bemused sales assistant. I would feel awkward as the sales assistant gave him her biggest fake smile, probably thinking that I was a lucky bitch, while I slunk into the shadows sheepishly, feeling like some kind of kept woman.

'Another pressie!' Tab would laugh, peering at my latest piece. 'Big again? That man has money to burn! Be careful, Amanda! Never trust a man who showers a woman with expensive gifts.'

'You're just jealous because you can't even afford Country Road on sale!' I'd reply, grinning, nudging her elbow.

No, Tab misunderstood Big. He was just generous; just very, very generous. No man had ever given me expensive tasteful gifts like he did. *No man*. And even I had to admit that I was beginning to get used to it.

I was beginning to feel like I was his.

I was under no illusions that I was becoming addicted to this man. Which went against every single rule in the How to Be a Good Escort manual. (There isn't one, by the way; that's my next book.)

We had a little routine: I'd fly to Melbourne every fortnight to tour as Samantha and he would be waiting on level 3 of the airport's short-term car park in his small and sleek navy Porsche, wearing his Prada sunglasses and a slick suit.

'Amanda,' he'd murmur, taking off his glasses to look at me.

'Big ...'

And we would kiss passionately in the front seat of his car, my legs parted, his hand sliding along my inner thigh, gently stroking my pussy over my panties.

We would last until Brunswick, where we would stop for lunch at some bustling Italian restaurant. But before that we would drive into some quiet underground car park and fuck furiously on the bonnet of his car; or, if it was busy, I would drop to my knees and suck him off with the windows closed and the air con on. It was frantic, fast, savage sex. It was the kind of sex people think escorts have, but we rarely do. It was actually the kind of sex you have when you are having an affair, but we weren't. We were addicted to each other. It was as simple as that.

So he'd invited me to Italy, to Lake Como. And it was amazing. Probably one of the most romantic places I have ever visited. But that was because I was with him.

The hotel was small, intimate and very, very expensive. Only the crème de la crème of European society were guests, plus a few loud-mouthed rich Americans. There were obscenely wealthy couples, spoilt children dressed head to toe in Missoni, wealthy old men with beautiful young Russian prostitutes, and me and Big.

'This is sensational, Big,' I gasped when we arrived, dropping my suitcase on the marble floor, peering through the oval window of our bedroom to the serene calm waters of Lake Como. 'This is *absolutely* sensational.'

'Fit for my princess,' Big smiled, taking me into his arms. And, although smelly and dirty and exhausted from our long-haul flight, we made love on the velvety-smooth white sheets of the finest Egyptian threads before falling asleep in each other's arms, exhausted.

We woke briefly hours later, in darkness except for the glow of light from the pool area beneath us, with the gentle samba of the band playing below and the warm laughter of other guests and the clinking of glasses.

We looked at each other and smiled, and I nuzzled even further into his body, as if trying to climb inside him.

'I'm going to write about this moment one day,' I whispered in his ear. And that was the moment I knew. That single moment, while the band swayed so gently and the moonlight danced on our marble floor, that was when I knew. My fragile heart, which had been hurt so many times before, was his. I was going to marry this man. Whatever it would take, I would do it. Samantha was going to get married.

CHAPTER 8

SAMANTHA

Mr No Name

One night, after I made my client squirt all over his iPad as we watched porn (I always went for the Old Man and Young Blonde category, god knows why – maybe because that seemed to be my life. I've seen more droopy old bums than I have young ones), we lay back in each other's arms with a nice glass of red. 'So, you know I'm in the middle of writing my second book, darling,' I said slowly, picking out a tiny bit of fluff from his belly button and inspecting it.

'Yes, Samantha …'

'Well, what do you want to be called?' I said. 'Clearly I have to write a chapter on you as you're such a big part of Samantha's life. So – choose your name!'

He laughed – a deep, throaty, wheezy laugh thanks to more than thirty years of smoking cigarettes and quaffing two bottles of red wine every evening.

Then, a pause.

'How about Mr Gullible?' he replied seriously.

'No! I'm not calling you that!' I shrieked, hitting him playfully. 'You're too nice to be called that! I meant something like Jon or Don ...'

'No, that's what I want you to call me, Samantha. I want you to call me Mr Gullible.'

I shook my head; there was no way I was going to call him Mr Gullible. That wasn't a nice name, and he was very, very sweet. He never cancelled, never asked for discounts and was always very accommodating, plus sex was never a big part of the booking. Every time he came to Sydney we would enjoy a lovely dinner (although he ate like a bird, preferring copious amounts of red wine to food). I, on the other hand, would plough my way through oysters, steak, French fries and Champagne while nodding along eagerly to his tales, which, if truth be told, I had heard many, many times before. We would then go back to his hotel for fumbling foreplay and cuddling, and fall asleep holding hands (well, with me trying to resist smothering him with a pillow after his guttural snores woke me up every half an hour).

In the morning he'd carefully place a cup of steaming coffee on the bedside table and peck my cheek before turning the shower on. His motto was that he 'never wakes a lady', and he doesn't (instead his snoring ensures they never sleep), but the smell of the coffee and the sound of the water jets from the luxury shower for two always do.

Sitting up in bed, I'd watch him get ready for work, gulp down his coffee (always Nescafé, which surprises me as this man was worth hundreds of millions), and pack up his battered rucksack (another surprise – this man has Louis Vuitton bags at home but chooses his battered rucksack because it allows him 'to carry two bottles of red wine into hotel rooms without anyone noticing').

Looks-wise he is no George Clooney, but he is a kind man and that makes him attractive in my eyes. He is small, with fluffy white hair and baby-soft skin (that more often than not smells of smoke) and a passion for historical battles, 'ladies' and extremely expensive hotel suites. I would always smile as we'd walk from the hotel lifts to his room, knowing, as our feet trod on the patterned carpet, that we would reach the door furthest away, in the corner, with the words 'Presidential Suite' or 'Deluxe Executive Suite' emblazoned on some sign, and it would be his.

So what could I call him? Mr Money Bags? No: despite the fancy rooms, he wasn't flash. The Shagger? No, he wasn't one of those. He was gentle, and preferred cuddling and foreplay to dirty sex (I was the one who encouraged the latter).

The Charmer? Yes, he was charming and sweet, and always made you feel you were lovely and special. But he wasn't slick enough to be The Charmer.

He was actually more of a storyteller. The first time I met him, in one of Sydney's most luxurious hotels, he opened his mouth to talk and I don't think he closed it again until he went to sleep (and then it wasn't really closed as he snored half the night).

He told me he had been seeing ladies for years, having discovered them quite accidentally when he punched in the words 'dinner date Sydney' into his iPad when alone on a business trip.

'All I wanted was a dinner companion!' he exclaimed gleefully, taking a big glug of shiraz that seemed to stain his teeth with every gulp. 'But then I realised there was this whole secretive world of ladies that I had no idea existed.'

After that, he was like a kid in a candy shop. He decided to enlist the company of ladies every time he travelled – which, of course, happened a lot more regularly than in his world pre-ladies. Suddenly dull conventions about the latest technology in porcelain toilet seats became *very* important to attend, particularly if the convention was in Las Vegas or Singapore or London, or anywhere else far, far away from his home, his wife and his real life in the countryside of New South Wales.

But it hadn't been all glitz and glamour during his foray into the escorting world. Mr No Name had endured his fair share of, shall we say, conwomen.

One 'lady' sponged thousands of dollars from him for her father's illness, then her mother's illness, then her dog's injury – and then asked him to cough up for the funeral costs of said dead mother, father and dog, who miraculously all happened to have popped their clogs – and paws – within the same month.

'I liked to give her the benefit of the doubt and paid for them all, but I told her I wanted nothing to do with her again,' he told me.

'Oh, you didn't pay for it all, did you?' I asked, shocked. 'Oh come on, surely not! Really, darling? But why?'

He nodded, looking at me sadly. 'Because I'm gullible, Samantha! What a fool I was,' he replied, taking another glug of shiraz. 'But I was a novice then. I was just trying to be helpful. I didn't know the rules and was scared that maybe she would blackmail me and tell my wife.'

What a cow, seriously. I'd love to know who she was, but my client wouldn't tell me. It was hard not to feel protective of him and his sweet naivety. Pretty stupid career move to be a conwoman escort – the industry is too small, surely?

Another 'lady' met up with him in the bar of a five-star hotel where they enjoyed fine wine and … not much else, as she snuck a few strong sleeping pills into his drink. He woke up the next day with no recollection of what had happened, and was left with nothing except a blinding headache as his wallet, watch and all his cash were gone.

'She'd even taken everything from the minibar,' he complained, shaking his head. 'Every single thing, even the bottled water. Do you know how embarrassing it was when the hotel staff asked whether I'd had anything from the minibar? I had to say, "Yes, I've had everything. Every single bloody thing." And to top it all off, she took a crap in my toilet and didn't even flush it.'

I shook my head, again in disbelief. How can so much bad luck happen to one lovely man? (And how can you not flush a toilet? But that's a different matter altogether.)

Still, his experiences didn't make him bitter, just wiser. He was still a very generous man. Every trip I accompanied him on, he would upgrade me to First Class while he sat in Business.

'A glass of red and then I sleep all the way! I'd just waste all that food,' was his excuse, but in truth he was simply very kind and liked to impress.

On the way back from Los Angeles once, while he was slumming it in Business, I made friends with half the businessmen in First Class. I've always thought planes are good places to meet potential clients; from the moment I glide into the Business Lounge at the airport (being a proud Platinum member was a pass card to meet more successful men, in my eyes), I often end up in conversation with some travelling man in a smart suit. (I'm waiting for my invitation to the Chairman's Lounge.) And when the question of 'And what do you do for work?' comes up, as it always does, I am always, *always* honest. Refreshingly so.

'Oh, I work in the sex industry,' I reply, my eyes dancing at their varying expressions, from clearly shocked, to amused, to excited – but mostly intrigued.

'I am a high-class escort ... Oh, you'd like my card? There you go, that's me, Samantha ... I have an agency too ...' Their eyes light up for those precious few moments they are being invited into a secret world. Then invariably, hours later, a text will pop up.

Hi Samantha, we met at the Business Lounge at Qantas. What a fascinating conversation! I happen to be coming to Sydney next week and wondered whether you might be free?

That's probably why I keep being honest with people – women included. Not because I need the work, to hustle.

But because I've never had a bad reaction – not to my face, anyway. So why should I lie to protect other people? There is only one way this industry will be destigmatised and that is if people understand that the men and women who work in it are actually pretty normal; that we do things like sit in airport lounges in our jeans and drink coffee; that we don't walk around in rubber catsuits (in public, at least), with black bendy dildos poking out of our handbags and needles out of our arms. Mind you, a very good escort friend of mine still blushes when she tells me about the time her bag was searched at security, and the male officer tried not to laugh as he pulled out giant vibrator after giant vibrator. (That was a rookie error. Rule number 101 of touring escorts: the boxes of condoms, lube and sex toys must always – I repeat, ALWAYS – be packed in the big suitcase ... and not left behind in the hotel room as tends to happen to me. Saying that, though, I never carry anything exciting with me: I only own one vibrator that collects dust in my drawer.)

We *choose* to do this, rather than slog our guts out forty hours a week for not much money and never seeing our kids. It's not for everyone, I get that. But it is for some. And the ones who do it, who I know, bloody love it.

Even my little trips to and from Melbourne saw me end up with a few extra business cards in my wallet. Once I sat next to an Orthodox Jew and we bonded after I told him that his kosher supper looked nicer than mine. Another time, a very well-dressed, portly man with a red face sat next to me in Business Class to Melbourne. He was pretending to watch his Louis Theroux documentary on his iPad when I kept catching him staring at my breasts.

'And what exciting plans do you have in Melbourne, young lady?' he drooled, his eyes again flitting to my nipples just as our trays were being taken away, and his face even redder after the two bottles of red wine he'd consumed mid-air.

'Oh me? Nothing much. Just going to the casino to take part in a gang bang,' I replied, barely blinking, thanking the air hostess as I passed her my rubbish. 'You?'

His beady eyes nearly popped out of his now-sweaty head as he crushed his water bottle with his fumbling hands.

'Oh ... oh my ... umm ... really? Oh gosh ... um ... well ... certainly nothing as exciting as what you're doing ... unfortunately ... very unfortunately ...' He spent the rest of the flight covering his hardened crotch with his iPad.

Another time, a very handsome, well-dressed man (from Melbourne, of course) was waiting at the gate for me after we'd both made our way off the plane. He stopped me as I walked past.

'Excuse me, can I just say that you are one of the most elegant women I have seen,' he said with confidence, his steely, determined blue eyes staring into mine. 'My name's Scott. Can I take you for dinner one evening?' (I mean, would that happen on a Tiger Airways flight? Would it?)

Dinner became sex became dating, and we spent a few lovely months seeing each other before we had a fight about something stupid and I tearfully slammed his bedroom door so ferociously that I broke his door handle. And that was the end of that. Turned out he loved my elegance and London accent but wasn't a fan of my Middle Eastern temper.

So that's why I only ever fly Qantas: not just because I trust the pilots (which I do, with my life) but because you always meet a *better class* of gentleman on a Qantas flight. And while many things I am not, a terrible snob I am.

Anyway, back to Mr No Name, the storyteller – I went on my very first overseas trip with him as an escort to Los Angeles, where he had to attend a few business meetings. I had the luxury of using his driver, Wally, for the times when my client was at work.

Every morning Mr No Name would leave me $500 spending money, and my days were spent walking aimlessly around the shops and buying gifts for my kids. (I always say the most dangerous thing about having a mother who's an escort is that the kids get spoilt.)

On the afternoon he had off he insisted on taking me to the Beverly Hills shopping centre where I was to 'walk into any shop and choose what I want'. Gucci, Chanel, Hervé Leger ... all the big glitzy names were at my – and his wallet's – disposal.

'Anything, Samantha, you can have anything you want,' he said, smiling triumphantly as we linked arms walking around the shops, our shoes clicking on the polished floors.

I felt awkward as he picked up handbags worth thousands of dollars and held them so I could have a proper look. I mean, of course they were gorgeous, but I had never been a labels girl. Five thousand dollars for a bag? I just couldn't justify it – even if it wasn't my money.

'You know what, I actually don't need anything, you sweet man,' I said, my eyes gazing at the sparkling bags, drawn to the diamond encrusting that gently caught the light. 'That bag is lovely, but really, I don't need it. Thank you, though. Why don't we go and have a coffee? Those doughnuts we saw looked amazing too ...'

And it was true: I didn't need some designer bag. I had mouths to feed, bills and a mortgage to pay. How could I justify a $5000 bag hanging up in my bedroom? Look, I'm no martyr: I drive a nice car; I always stay in five-star hotels, I like to upgrade to Business Class when I can. I like nice things. But $5000 on a bag?

I had clearly upset him, though. His kind eyes crumpled and I felt like I'd just elbowed him in the guts.

'But *all* the ladies like shopping!' he replied, clearly confused. 'One lady made me buy her a twenty-thousand-dollar purse on Rodeo Drive *and* I paid her son's school fees.' While he was telling me another sad tale of yet another greedy woman pilfering his cash, it was hard not to think that maybe, just maybe, I *should* be calling him Mr Gullible – or Mr Stupid, more like. I don't care so much about what other ladies do or don't do – give someone like that enough rope and they will hang themselves. But I know I don't need or want these things, because that's all they are: things.

I'd already charged him an extortionate fee for my company on this trip (no, I'm not telling you how much but I will say it was equal to four months' wages when I was a journalist). I just didn't need a Gucci bag on top of it. (Although I am writing this – on a plane to Guess Where. Looking at my tatty old bag, I am wondering why the bloody hell I didn't take the offer of a new one.)

'Darling, you have already spent a lot of money on me during this trip,' I explained, hoping I didn't sound ungrateful or rude. 'And you flew me First Class and I really don't need anything, really.'

'Please, Samantha,' he said. 'I would really like to buy something for you.'

It was going to be hard to get out of this one, I could see that. Mr No Name clearly wanted to spend money on his lady and I was worried that if I resisted anymore, he would take grave offence and I would be on the bottom of his list of favourite ladies. He'd told me, over (another) glass of red the night before, that I was currently sitting comfortably in the top-three division.

'Who's number one?' was my obvious question.

'Shhh, I'm not telling you!' he smiled, taking a huge sip of shiraz and tapping my knee in mock annoyance. 'You are such a journalist, Samantha! You know that's what I call you, don't you? The Journalist!'

Journalist maybe, but I could also be called The Animal Lover. I had two dogs and two cats at home that my housesitter, Alice, was minding. I use the description 'housesitter' loosely and reluctantly, as Alice is far more than staff – she is the closest thing I have to family in Sydney. We met and bonded while she was a sales assistant in a local shop, always happy, always smiling and always doing anything for anybody.

Alice's kindness puts us all to shame. She takes gifts at Christmas to the lonely old men in the local retirement home, even though she struggles financially, and she knows all the names of the homeless people in our area. When serious illness befell her she soldiered on bravely and silently, barely missing a day of work, refusing help and driving herself to doctors' appointments. She is a proud, strong woman.

'I'm used to doing things alone,' she told me once after my offer to help was rebuffed yet again. 'I don't like to be a bother.'

When chemotherapy was ravaging her tiny body and angry red scars formed where aggressive skin cancers had been sliced out, she put on her cheery face and carried on.

'I'm a very lucky woman, Amanda. It's a beautiful day and I'm happy to be alive,' she said brightly, scanning my shopping at the till, neatly arranging the items in a plastic bag. 'Anyway, more importantly, how are *you*, love?'

When the shop was taken over by new owners and a devastated Alice was out of a job, I couldn't think of a better person to be my housesitter/dog walker/cleaner.

Now in her mid-forties, she still gets up at 2 a.m. every day to drive all the way from her home in the far depths of western Sydney to the place she really calls home: Bondi Beach, where she grew up. You'll find her running laps of the beach at 4 a.m. before she starts her cleaning jobs at the local shops, units and homes. You can't walk down the road with her without every local stopping her to ask how she is.

Every time I travel or go on tour, she stays at mine to mind my pets and, more importantly, she gets to lie in past 2 a.m.

'Do you think I could be one of your escorts?' she will joke, trying on my Louboutins, click-clacking on my floorboards.

'You wish!' I joke back, giving her a nudge. 'Get your stinky feet out of my shoes!'

Since the second my Rottweiler, Rosie, took a liking to her – as most living creatures do – Alice has been like family to me.

And if there was one special person in my life who would appreciate a $5000 Gucci bag, it was Alice.

'I'll do a deal,' I told Mr No Name. 'I'll let you buy me that bag if you let me give it to a woman who I know would really appreciate it. I want to get her a gift and you would be doing me a huge favour by buying it for me. How does that sound?'

'That sounds very fair,' he smiled, and eagerly took the very expensive bag to the very happy sales assistant behind the counter. Then he gave it to me, and I gave it to a very shocked Alice back home.

'Yes, it's real, before you ask!' I grinned, handing it to her and watching her eyes light up.

'You're bloody joking! Amanda, seriously! That is so generous of you!' she exclaimed breathlessly, her hard-working fingers opening every secret section of the leather finery. 'A real Gucci bag! I've only admired bags like these in fancy magazines … Bloody hell, I want your job!'

'Oh, it wasn't me, Alice, I can't take credit for it. I didn't buy it, it was my client. He bought it for you.'

'God bless him! What a sweet man, what a kind soul. I'll have to send him a little card, won't I? What's his name? Now where's my pen?' And she scrabbled inside her plastic bag, pulling out some scrap of paper at the same time.

I looked at her and for a second I was lost for words. So what was I going to call this man?

'Let's just call him Mr, um, Mr …'

'Yes? Mr what?' she replied, her pen tapping.

'Let's just call him Mr Nice.'

CHAPTER 9

AMANDA

PCM, NOK and other lonely acronyms

Well, Italy had sealed the deal: Mr Big and I were officially 'in love'. We sat close to each other on the flight home, holding hands all the way.

'I can't stand you working anymore,' he said, turning to face me as the tyres on the Qantas Airbus A380 finally skidded on the steamy tarmac back in Australia. 'I just can't bear it, Amanda – I can't stomach the thought of other men touching you. Whatever it takes, I'll do it.'

I blinked silently, looking at his pleading eyes and his beautiful face, now tanned and relaxed. I thought back to our holiday: to the limoncello we drank until our cheeks flushed; the candles we lit in churches so old the dusty walls were crumbling and the ethereal light streamed in through brightly coloured glass; the balmy nights we made love in twisted sheets until the morning sun slowly warmed our bodies.

As the plane jolted to a halt and everyone rushed to unclick their belts, Big and I sat there for a few moments.

So he didn't want me to see other men. Well, that was a pretty big statement, wasn't it? No more Samantha.

No more Samantha?

As if I would do that! You know how much I loved Samantha. She gave me money – and freedom. Any single mother will tell you that flexibility is the biggest drawcard. Mine was a damn good job for a woman my age (I've stopped telling people my age, by the way – a friend of mine in the industry scolded me about it once. She's forever thirty-something when she's really pushing mid-forties. 'That's fine,' I replied smartly. 'But I'd rather look good for forty then old for twenty-nine,' before making a mental note that, yes, she was probably right, and I stopped telling people my age from that day onwards).

But it wasn't just the money and the hours: Samantha was exciting; she was fun; she was my best friend. And what would her clients say? Lovely English Mark, Mr Nice ...? She cared for them very much, and –

'I don't want to do it either,' I found myself saying quietly, squeezing his hand. 'I would love to see only you.'

And I also loved Big.

I didn't want to lose him. I had found someone special – rather, he had found me – and it's not every day that happened. I was fussy; I rarely liked a man enough to date him. I nitpicked and found little things that put me off. But Big? There was nothing. I loved everything about this man. From his face to his smell to his voice. I loved his brains and his body. And I *really* loved his cock.

So I found myself agreeing to give up escorting and for Big to be the only one.

Just. Like. That.

'Great,' he said, breaking into a relieved smile. 'Will XXX a month be enough for you?'

I'm not going to disclose how much he agreed to pay me. Not to protect myself from the tax man – because, again, I pay enough tax. (In fact, every time my tax bill comes in I keep telling myself that I need to find a more dodgy accountant.) But while I don't mind telling you about our sex, or his gifts or our conversations, his money situation – how much he's got or hasn't got – is private. Men may not mind the world knowing how big their manhood is, but they don't want the world to know how much is in their bank accounts.

I will say, though, that while his offer was generous, and it would cover my expenses as well as give me a bit extra, it wasn't silly money. It wasn't enough for me to lead the life I had been accustomed to.

Since becoming Samantha I had swapped my old Subaru for a convertible BMW. I had nice furniture, and went on nice holidays – always five star. If I needed a break I wouldn't think twice about booking myself on a retreat for a week and not getting much change from $5000. Escorting is like an ATM – it's the gift that keeps giving. You have quiet days and weeks, feast or famine, panic about money and think a client will never book you again, that your glory days as an escort have passed. And then, out of nowhere, the clients reappear and the cash flows in again.

But when it came to Big's offer, that didn't matter. I could economise. I wouldn't need to travel so much now, would I? I didn't need to jet off around the country seeing clients. I didn't need to buy so many clothes and lingerie. Did I really need those hair extensions all the time if I wasn't working? Think of all the money I could save! Big's offer was a good one – and I accepted.

We called it our PCM deal (per calendar month). 'I'm doing this for you, darling,' was his reasoning. 'You need to stop escorting. And I want to help you.'

The deal was that Big would support me and I would stop seeing clients. I'd have to pull all my advertising, stop doing any media, definitely not write a second book. I could still have my agency – as long as my face wasn't pictured, he said – but that was it. One day, eventually, I'd get a normal job like everyone else and we could pretend this thing of me coming out to the bloody world as an escort was some big joke – a midlife crisis. Big kept telling me that 'time heals everything'. Like I had committed some terrible crime and done ten years in prison – and, don't worry, everyone will forget it ... or at least let's hope they do.

His favourite word became 'time'. As time passed, he promised, I'd meet his friends, his kids, his work colleagues. I'd be part of his life, not just a secret in hotel rooms.

'It will take time,' he kept saying. 'It won't happen overnight.' But that was okay; I could wait. Big had kids he saw regularly, an ex-wife, a respectable job; he couldn't just introduce me, an escort with a public profile, into his life. Not everyone was accepting of my job; I understood that.

It was worth waiting for, the carrot he was dangling. That bit – the family bit – was the part that was the most attractive. I would have some security – not financial, because it wasn't so much about the money. I could make in a week what he was offering to give me for the month. But like I said, it wasn't about the money.

What it was, finally, was having a NOK. No, that is not some strange sex-related acronym. Instead, quite simply, I finally had someone to write as my Next of Kin. That horrible bit on a medical form where you have to write down who to call in an emergency. Your parents, your partner, your sibling – they're probably *your* next of kin. You probably have so many family members to choose from! I am pretty sure not having a NOK would be something that wouldn't ever cross your mind.

But it did mine – because I didn't really have one. Australia wasn't the country I grew up in. My school friends lived in London, as did my sister.

My best friend Tab lived in Melbourne.

My parents and I were estranged.

I didn't have a partner.

I couldn't exactly put down a client.

Was I the only person in the whole bloody country who didn't have a NOK?

Do the inventors of these forms not understand that in an emergency, some people have no one to call? Or that some people actually don't *want* to call anyone?

Is that space on the form just a way of testing whether you are truly loved or not? It should read: 'Okay, do you have any family that you are still speaking to and, if so, do you know their phone number off by heart?'

So when I stumbled across the NOK part of a form – which I do quite often, being partial to a doctor's appointment or two in my life – my pen would always hover over the black line.

Could I have put my neighbour at number 12? We fell out once over a mop (don't ask) but I went round the next day with beers to say sorry (I may have a temper, but I always apologise) and we got on fine. Still, I didn't think he would jump at the chance to face Sydney rush-hour traffic to bring me a cheese sandwich in hospital.

Or could I have asked Reuven, the owner of my local cafe, Skinny Dip? He lent me a ladder once; I'm sure he would have done it. Would he have minded if he was my NOK? More importantly, would his wife have minded?

Alice would have done it but she had her own family and kids to worry about, plus she lived a million miles away from me and I felt she already did so much for me. My best male friend, Remington, kept offering, but I was always picking *him* up from his latest cosmetic procedure, plus his boyfriend had just moved with him, so I'd probably never see him again.

So, sometimes, I just left that bit blank, or I would write 'n/a'. *Don't call anyone. I'll be fine. There are no loved ones to call. It's just me.*

And once in a while – not often, but if I was feeling emotional – tears would well up in my eyes.

So while I did love Big and I loved being with him, the main drawcard for me accepting the PCM was the NOK and the things that were going to come with that: being part of someone's life again; having family meals with our blended kids, and going on lovely holidays together. It was, after all, just a matter of time before I was able to be introduced as Amanda, his partner. It was time. Just that. A little bit of time.

'Anything you want, just ask,' he kept saying. 'And I will put the money into your bank account.'

But you'd also know by now that this wouldn't be easy for me. To ask for money! I do have pride. But I did as he asked, reluctantly.

'Um, my mortgage payment is due this week, darling,' I would stammer over the phone, cringeing.

'Yep, how much do you need?' he would reply. He would be busy at work; I could hear typing and phones ringing.

'Um, whatever you think, darling.'

And, true to his word, a few thousand dollars would appear in my account the next day. He never didn't pay, he never complained, never raised an eyebrow, never said no.

How easy was that? What a deal this was! Surely it was every escort's dream – wasn't I being rescued? Wasn't I being plucked from the dire depths of this degrading world of seedy prostitution by a handsome rich American on a white horse? If you squinted, and if the room was dark enough, he even looked like Richard Gere.

I'm sure you're thinking it was coup of the century, as you're reading this on the bus on a rainy Monday morning while I'm being paid to literally do nothing – except not work. I was a kept woman.

But I hated it. I absolutely hated asking him – or anyone, for that matter – for money. Give me the floppy, flaccid penis of some obese engineer to excite any day of the week. I'd rather have sex with that than ask someone for money.

Then one day I was sitting anxiously at a new clinic, waiting to have laser treatment to get rid of the small tattoo I'd had done when I was eighteen and stupid: a rose on my left breast. The bigger my boobs got, the more ridiculous that rose looked. And as an escort your boobs only go one way – up.

'Would you mind filling these out while you're waiting and Doctor Anthony won't be too much longer,' said the young pretty brunette behind the counter with a smile, as she handed me a black clipboard.

'Not a problem.'

And there, after I'd answered all the questions about what medication I was on, and had I read the consent forms and did I have epilepsy (no – but did mood swings count?) and blah blah, came the question I'd been waiting for.

Who do we call in an emergency?

Well! That bit was easy now. My pen excitedly, proudly and very carefully wrote the letters in my neatest writing with the Grace Kelly (limited edition) Montblanc pen he'd bought me. And those words were:

Mr Big.

Just writing those two little words made me have a sense of belonging. Of being loved and cared for. And that's all Amanda ever really wanted, deep down.

CHAPTER 10

SAMANTHA

The perils of being an (almost) famous high-profile escort

Here are three questions I get asked all the time:

1) What has life been like since going public as an escort?
2) Can you help me be an escort?
3) Do you have sex all the time?

The answers are:

1) You are reading about it now.

2) I mentor women to become escorts but am getting tired of the dumb ones (and it's only the dumb ones) pinching my ideas and abusing my kindness.

3) No.

Yep, the answer to number three is a big fat *no*. I DO NOT HAVE MUCH SEX. Since going public as an escort/journalist I reckon I have less sex now than ever before. I know you won't believe me, but it's true. I had more sex as a journalist. I would estimate that a single mum in her forties – or any woman, really (except the young hot ones because they're always bonking) – who is on Tinder would have much more sex than me. And that's not because I am not working – I am – but because clients, especially new ones, treat me differently now. Without wanting to sound like a big-headed hooker (I think there are a few out there), when men book me now it is more out of curiosity than to relieve a twitchy cock. It is more to do with meeting this 'Samantha X' and finding out what makes her tick (um, French Champagne and a fat envelope stuffed full of cash?).

One word I hear daily from men is that I am 'intriguing'. I could be sitting next to a businessman on a flight to, ooooooh, let's say Melbourne, and after a brief chat he will say: 'Wow, you are so *intriguing*.'

Or Sean my window cleaner will shake his head while laughing at my stories.

'You're bloody joking! He didn't say that, did he?' he'd say while wiping spiders' webs from my sliding doors with a big, wet sloppy cloth. 'I love your stories, Amanda. They're so *intriguing*!'

I have clients who are writing books and want me to proofread them in my spare time (SPARE time!!).

'I'm up to my fourth draft,' mumbled Andrew in between chewing his avocado toast over brunch the other day. 'It's only just over a hundred thousand words. I've emailed it to you, so when you get a chance, can you have a quick look for me?'

A quick 100 000 words? Sure, no problem …

Or dear Keith, who is writing his escorting memoirs and I rarely have time to help him (sorry, Keith!).

Or I'll get an email from a client and it will read like this. In fact, it will read *exactly* like this as this is a real email (name changed, of course).

Dear Samantha,
I have to say I read your book on a flight to
New York recently and felt compelled to write to
you. Your story is fascinating and I must say, I
find you intriguing. I am from London originally,

but have been living in Sydney for over 20 years.
I am a lawyer who has also lived in Hong Kong
and New York. I confess that I have wanted to
explore the possibility of seeing you for some
time but I was a little nervous given you are ...
well, let's be honest, now so well-known. But
my intrigue has got the better of me. Would you
happen to be free for dinner next Tuesday night?
Cash no issue.
Yours, Fraser.

Before coming out I used to get emails like this:

R U free? Can U wear black suspenders and do U
swallow? Ben.

For the record, I did meet with Fraser and he was lovely.
And in our four-hour meeting we had very pleasant sex
once, for nine minutes, and that was right at the beginning.
The rest of the time we talked. (And as for Ben: no, I don't
swallow and FK OFF.)

I find that these days men are more interested in talking
to me than having sex with me. And you may find it hard
to believe that I often find myself leaving appointments
feeling sexually frustrated, sometimes cursing the fact I

ever wrote that bloody book. Instead of feeling refreshed, elated and relaxed after a marathon sex session with a nice man, I'd usually depart a hotel room feeling like I'd just done a Q and A and book-signing session.

Take a dear regular, Lee. He was young, with a big head of frizzy hair and a weakness for working girls, and he had been a client with my agency since the day we launched. He would always buy the girls a gift and the girls loved him.

'Such an easy guy, so lovely – the sex is great!' I always heard as feedback from my girls. He was a pleasure to deal with and he was always so polite to me.

One day, I'll pluck up the courage to see you, Samantha! The big boss! he kept texting.

And that day finally arrived. He was so nervous I thought he was going to pass out. I tried to kiss him but his lips were trembling so much.

'Sorry, Samantha,' he said, scratching his head. 'I am really confused. I've never been with a celebrity before. I don't know whether to feel horny or starstruck.'

I had to laugh. Is that how clients saw me: a celebrity? It was very sweet – if only my sex life didn't have to suffer.

'Celebrities need sex too, Lee,' I said, climbing on top of his shaking body.

Or there was Cam, the truckie who booked me for an hour at his city hotel one December afternoon. I knew that when I clapped eyes on him standing by the lifts, I was going to have the best sex of my life. It had been ages since I'd had sex, and the sun was out, it was Christmas time, I was in a good mood ...

Cam wasn't attractive at all, but you'd know by now that attractiveness rarely matters. I can have the best sex with the most unattractive men – and it's usually those kinds of men who make me orgasm. Most escorts say the same thing: give us a man with a face only his mother could love and we will have great sex. Maybe we relax more? Maybe we actually like them as people more? Maybe we feel more powerful, more in control? A good-looking client just makes me nervous. A good-looking client who is an arrogant dickhead is the worst kind of client; any girl will tell you that.

Anyway, Cam was bald and stocky with a moustache which had a bit of cheese in it (I think it was cheese). He was wearing a gold chain, a red checked shirt and these big, chunky workmen's boots.

'G'day, Samantha!' He beamed, opening the lift doors and marching in before me. He lacked decorum, he was brash and rough around the edges.

Perfect. All the ingredients for a good bonk.

When we got to the tiny studio room I put my bag down and went to kiss him. 'Well, hello, Cam! You're in trouble today ...' I whispered seductively into his hairy ear.

'Er, rightio!' he choked out, sounding petrified. 'But before we get down to that, I suppose I'd better offer you a drink. Now, what do we have here ... I don't think there's much ...'

'Whatever you've got would be lovely,' I murmured patiently. A glass of bubbles wouldn't hurt to get me in the mood – not that I needed it.

I watched as Cam plodded to the bathroom, fetched the plastic cup that his toothbrush had been in, filled it up with warm tap water and handed it to me, grinning.

'Here we go, love,' he said nervously, passing me the cup with shaking hands. 'Water looks a bit cloudy, if you ask me, but I think that's because it's warm.'

'Oh, it's fine,' I smiled, putting the cup down. Well, that was a first. But I wasn't here for the drink ...

'Now let me give *you* something ...'

I unclipped the straps of my dress and let it fall to my feet sexily, standing there in all my glory, showing Cam my body that was aching to be devoured. *Surely* he was aching to devour me ...

'Oh jeez, Samantha,' he stammered, looking away. 'I don't mean to be rude but ...'

He reached out into his rucksack, fumbling around.

Jesus Christ – this was it: my first psychopath! He looked a bit like Ivan Milat, he drove trucks on dusty orange freeways ... What was he getting – a gun, a knife ...

Nope.

My *book*.

A well-thumbed copy of *Hooked* that he held out to me with a proud expression on his face.

'I bought a copy of your book, love. Would you mind putting your clothes back on and signing it for me? I've been dying to meet you to find out how life has been for you since you did that show on TV ... I have so many questions for you. I actually wrote some down here on this piece of paper. We saw you on Channel Seven – or was it Nine – my missus and me, and ...'

I stared at his mouth moving and his eyes blinking excitedly. Remind me again why I wrote that bloody book?

CHAPTER 11

AMANDA

No power in love

I don't know what Frankie from Frankie Goes to Hollywood was going on about when he sang about the Power of Love, because the more I fell in love with Big, the less power I seemed to have.

I wasn't used to this thing called 'love'. I wasn't used to having someone call me three times a day to check where I was, and I wasn't used to not working. More than that, I was becoming very, very clingy, and I certainly wasn't used to that. And neither was Mr Big.

The whole bloody point of me not working and being with Big was to feel more secure. But, in truth, I had never felt more insecure.

If I called him and he didn't answer, my mind would go into overdrive. *Is he with an escort? What's he doing? Why hasn't he called me back yet?*

Not only did we live in different states – so I spent nights wondering, worrying what he was getting up to – but I felt my self-confidence sliding. Not that I minded that he lived far away – I was quite relieved. While I was in love with him, I also loved my own space and my own time. But it played havoc with my jealousy ...

'Study something, start a business, concentrate on your writing,' Big would urge me. 'You're such a smart girl, you can do anything you like! Why you chose to escort I have no idea ... what a waste of talent ...'

This idea of not being *good enough* was becoming a theme.

My job as an escort was a major embarrassment; a major blot on my CV. I was somehow a lesser person, a lesser woman, for choosing sex work.

And so it went on. I would listen, at first trying to stick up for myself, to say that actually I *did* have a 'proper' career once, a really successful one as a journalist for many, many years – had he forgotten? That escorting was something I had chosen. Did he not remember?

Let's not forget that if I hadn't been an escort, I wouldn't have met Mr Big – The Peacock. Remember him? The man who had seen quite a few escorts in his time, including me? But we all know what men do is okay, because they're men! They can do what they want without being questioned, blamed or made to feel guilty. And god forbid a woman who does what the hell she wants with her body/life – we are labelled mad, selfish, crazy, sluts and so forth.

However, being told off for being Samantha was becoming a daily ritual. If the newspapers published one of my opinion pieces, he wouldn't talk to me for days. Then, once out of his sulk, a text message would pop up: *Proud of yourself again, are you? What absolute rubbish you write. When is this going to stop, Amanda? You are clearly addicted to working.*

I hosted an event in Sydney, a Q and A evening. Women who had travelled from all around the country had paid almost $100 to spend a few hours listening to me talk about Samantha, and they got to ask questions at the end. How did Big support me?

He didn't. The phone was silent.

There was no 'good luck', or congratulatory text message. No flowers waiting on my doorstep. For someone who called me or texted constantly to check my movements, I didn't hear from him for days.

'I just want it all to stop,' he snapped when I pulled him up on it. 'It has to stop. If you want to be with me, it has to stop.'

And the more often I would hear how it *had to stop*, the more I started to believe it. Maybe escorting really was a 'bad' thing to do? Big was correct: I shouldn't write for the press anymore. Maybe I *was* mad and crazy? I should fade into the background, I really should. I was a terrible person ... making terrible decisions ... What the fuck was I thinking, coming out to the public? What on earth had made me become an escort?

It didn't matter how many women were still writing to me in their hundreds wanting support and advice, or how many times Vanessa would give me pep talks about how she believed in me, I started to lose my *chutzpah*. My confidence completely evaporated.

Big had to be right: he was the voice of reason, wasn't he? A sensible businessman who wanted a sensible life. I *should* get a normal job. I was never going to have a nice, normal life with a nice man if I carried on working. Of course he was right!

There was no way I wanted to go back to an office, though. So I scrolled through university websites looking for a course to spark my interest. I looked at the requirements for becoming a Qantas flight attendant (seeing as I spent so much times on planes). I even considered working in a boutique in my local area, or becoming a florist.

Something sedate and sensible and socially acceptable: 'Meet Amanda, she's a florist.'

But my heart wasn't in it. I was torn – completely, utterly torn between wanting to be with the man I loved and have a life together, and being Samantha. Big was making me choose. And for now, love won.

Once I spent a whole week with him. I took his shirts to the dry cleaners, tidied up his hotel room, made sure there were fresh flowers and even bought him organic jelly beans – the jumbo ones – as I knew they were his favourite.

But he grumbled that it was a waste of money to put his shirts in when he could wash and iron them himself, told me I'd put the clean clothes in the wrong places and came home late from work a few nights.

He had all sorts of lotions or potions, from Chanel, Dior, or some expensive organic brand which I sometimes pinched, or I'd leave the top unscrewed.

'Amanda!' he'd say, exasperated. 'Buy your own!'

But then something would happen. I needed advice about something, or once, when I found a lump in my breast, he was on the next plane to Sydney. It turned out to be nothing, but he was there. He was always on the end of the phone if I needed to talk and even his voice relaxed me.

And we'd go to bed, and the sex ... the cuddles ... his smell ...

'I love you so much, Amanda,' he would always say at night and in the morning. 'And I want you to be mine.'

I would smile at the fact that I now belonged to him, wrap my body around his, nuzzle into his neck and whisper that I loved him too. Because I really did. I loved him.

———

It had been months since we had agreed to the PCM and I hadn't met any of his friends, work colleagues or family. I got that his separation was reasonably fresh; I got that I was a controversial figure; I got that he had an image to uphold – but not even a hint of acceptance? Not even an 'I'm seeing someone now' to his friends?

'Oh darling, Scott's calling,' I'd say, passing his phone, hoping that Mr Big would casually drop my name into the conversation. Scott was his business partner and best friend. But Big would take the phone and go to a quiet place and put his finger over his lips to *shush* me.

If his sisters called – and they did, daily, usually when we were driving – he would mostly ignore their calls.

'Pick it up, it could be urgent!' I'd say, turning the radio volume down.

'No, she can wait, I'll call her back later,' he'd reply, eyeing the name on the bluetooth but turning the music up again. And I would sit there stewing because, once more, he didn't want them to get a hint of me being around.

But when Big came to my home in Sydney, my life, my friends, I welcomed him with open arms. He dined with me at all my local eateries, met my friends, came to the gym with me and even walked my dogs when I was sick. I used to joke that he was pissing on my territory. He made sure he was seen with me everywhere in my local area, from cafes, to gyms, to restaurants – even insisting on driving my car. He wanted to be seen as mine, and I loved showing him off. I had no issue whatsoever introducing this man to Amanda's world because I loved him and wanted him to be a part of my life.

'Have you met his friends yet?' Tab asked one day and she looked at me. But we both knew the answer: no, of course I hadn't. I knew what she was thinking: that I never would.

'In time,' I replied. 'He said in time.'

She snorted, 'Get real, Amanda! You will never meet them. But my question to you is: can you cope with that? He's got you where he wants you and nothing will ever change for him. You shouldn't have given up your work for him so easily.'

Ouch.

But I knew she was probably right. Tab might sound harsh but she wasn't his biggest fan. She could see me slowly giving up my power, and apart from nice meals and gifts, she couldn't see me getting much in return.

Having been my friend for almost twenty years, she knew more than anyone how much I craved family and being part of something special.

However, I wasn't feeling very hopeful about being introduced to anyone, not even his local barista, any time soon. Exactly how much time was going to have to pass before I became acceptable? Until I had severed all ties from my escorting world, including my regulars? Until I was 100 years old with white whiskers sprouting from my chin? All that hard work Vanessa had put in helping me build my brand just gone, like that, because Big didn't like it?

'Keep believing people you pay,' he'd snort when I'd tell him of a great opportunity Vanessa wanted me to try. Like I was some kind of idiot. Like I was useless and stupid and had no one around who cared for me – apart from him. Of course, I knew he was trying to cause a rift between Vanessa and me, or trying to make me question my business. I just stayed silent. Mr Big was charming and handsome and nice to me, but even I knew he was also a jealous and insecure man. *Just his faults*, I'd tell myself. No one is perfect.

I had pulled my advertising and stopped seeing clients, as hard as that was. I hadn't made a big ding-dong about it – I'd just told my regulars quietly that I was having a break. I simply wasn't very available, and I certainly didn't take on any new clients. *Sorry – I'm not available but I do have plenty of Angels who are,* I'd text back, trying to encourage the man to see one of my girls.

And part of it, I admit, was quite nice. Big and I had cosy dinners and lie-ins in bed because I didn't have to rush off to a job, and he was extremely happy because he had me all to himself. It was nice not worrying where the next dollar was coming from, because I knew it would be from him, even though I had to ask for it; and the only place I needed to travel to was Melbourne to see him and to stay in our favourite hotel.

But there was something inside me that felt uneasy. I couldn't put my finger on it; I can't even explain it to you now. But it was just a feeling. An icky, yucky feeling in my tummy.

When I was feeling brave, I'd push the family thing and ask about his sisters. 'Maybe one Christmas we can spend it all together?' I asked hopefully one evening over dinner.

'Not yet, Amanda,' was his reply. 'One day, darling, but not yet.'

One evening, over espresso martinis at a bustling bar, I grabbed Big's phone and took a selfie of us smiling at the camera, and before Big could grab it back, I texted it to his sister.

'What the fuck, Amanda!' he yelped, snatching his precious phone from me. 'Why the fuck would you do that?'

'Why not?' I replied. 'It would be nice if one of your bloody sisters knew I existed.'

His sister texted back straightaway: *She's pretty. Who's she?*

Just some girl I just met in the bar. Being friendly, he wrote back, and moodily put his phone away.

'What's wrong with you, for Christ's sake?' he snapped.

My eyes pricked with tears. *Just some girl?* We had been together for months now. *Just some fucking girl?*

Another time, I'd had a few drinks with some friends and thought it would be a nice idea to surprise Big at his swish office. I was wearing a pink dress and heels, and looked like I could have been a business colleague.

'I'm in the lobby,' I announced, a bit tipsy and excited over the phone.

'You're what?' he hissed back quietly.

'I've come to surprise you! I'm downstairs in your building! Fancy a coffee?'

Minutes later, the lift went *ding-ding* and this man with anger and fear in his eyes swept out of the door, grabbed me by the elbow and led me outside.

'What the hell are you doing here?' Big demanded.

'I was in the city ... and ...'

'Come on, let's go for a walk.'

He was walking fast and in my heels it was hard to catch up.

'Amanda, don't touch me here,' he'd snap if I tried to hold his hand. 'This is where I work, for god's sake, people know me here.'

He led me to Chanel. 'Here, do you want something? Let me buy you something,' he said, his voice rising with panic, clearly on the lookout for people he knew. 'These sunglasses are nice – try them on? Or what about this jacket? This pair of shoes?'

'No, I'm fine … No, I don't want anything. I just wanted to see you!' I was beginning to sober up pretty quickly. Then, softly again, almost to myself, I said, 'I just wanted to see *you*, I don't need anything. Just you.'

'Okay, let me put you in a taxi, then'. He hailed a taxi, put me in with a nervous grin and slammed the door hard.

You're crazy but I love you, read the peacemaking text message he sent as my taxi pulled away.

Crazy? Really? Was it crazy of me to turn up to his work? Isn't that what couples do?

He loved me? Really? Was that love? Wanting to throw down a few thousand dollars in Chanel rather than have a $3.50 coffee with me in his local cafe? *Was that love?* Sure didn't feel like it to me.

What was I? An embarrassment to him? Was I that bad to be seen with? I was starting to feel mad and insecure and unloved and, yes, crazy. Whatever effect being with Big was having, it was no longer making me feel loved. It was hurting me– hurting me a lot.

Deep down, maybe I was testing him to see how he would react to me turning up at his work. And he failed that test. He didn't want me anywhere near his other life. He'd rather buy me thousands of dollars worth of Chanel than risk bumping into a work colleague in the street with me.

I didn't want Chanel. I wanted acceptance. To be loved. I thought that was our deal now. And still my clients were texting, wanting to see me. They wanted to be seen *with* me. I kept turning them down. And this was how I was treated in return?

It wasn't until a few nights later, at a fashionable new Chinese restaurant, that I asked him outright.

'Big, how long do you think it will be before you introduce me to your friends and family?' My voice was shaky and my eyes had already filled with tears. I think it was because I already knew the answer.

'I don't know, Amanda,' he replied, his eyes darting everywhere except to me. 'Why do you always do this? You always try to ruin it when we're together. We're having such a lovely night. That's why I love you – you're so crazy!

Now, do you fancy those small noodles or the big ones? I'm not that hungry, so …'

'No, Big – I want to know. If I am to give up Samantha and everything that comes with it, I have a right to know. I don't want any fucking noodles. Just tell me how long. Months? Years? How long do I have to wait?'

'For Christ's sake, Amanda,' he snapped, his eyes darting faster now. 'You're such hard work. No man would put up with you. I tell you, no other man would be as patient as me.'

'How long?' I said, my voice getting an octave higher. Big knew that with my Persian fire and my London mouth, I had no problem making a scene in public and my voice getting higher was a clear Code Red.

'Years, okay?' he hissed, looking at me, obviously angry now. 'Years. Satisfied? It's not easy for me. My family are traditional. They wouldn't approve. If only you hadn't written that book … Now, can we please enjoy our dinner? I think those thin noodles tonight, and a bottle of the pinot …' He summoned over the waiter as his voice trailed off.

I knew then. In that clattery, hip Chinese restaurant in Melbourne, with the rain belting down against the large glass windows, and the tears streaming down my face, with Big trying to comfort me, embarrassed at my public emotion, the kind waiter handing me serviettes while plonking steaming bowls of thin noodles down. I knew. That feeling of dread? It was real. TAKE-HOME TIP: Never ignore those feelings at the bottom of your tummy. They're never wrong. Your body never lies to you.

'What the hell was wrong with you tonight?' he asked as we climbed into his car.

'Nothing,' I mumbled, tears plop-plopping down, turning to face the other way. For fuck's sake! How the hell had I come to this? I'd become one of *those* women. Those victims. My neediness would send him into the arms of another woman, for sure.

'Just stop this, okay?' he said. 'Stop it. Just stop asking me stupid questions. I love you and I want to be with you – it's just going to take a bit of time. Time heals everything ...'

And as we drove along the busy roads, the glare of headlights stinging my red eyes, the questions I'd been asking myself had well and truly been answered.

I'd been a bloody fool.

It was never going to happen, was it? I was never going to meet his family. I was never going to have a big blended Christmas. I was never going to be the one he came home to after work or invited for dinner with his friends.

I was tarred; I had a black mark on me. I was a high-profile sex worker and author and, quite simply, that was not the kind of woman he wanted as a wife (but he clearly didn't want any other man to want me, either). I was never going to be *good enough.*

So what did Amanda do? She called on the person who knew how to take her female power back. A woman who would slip on her high heels and stomp on his heart, put on her lipstick and slip into that dress. She would sit at a bar, all eyes on her, meet her client and enjoy being the goddess for a few hours and a few thousand dollars. She would call on the woman who wouldn't put up with that crap from a man, who didn't even need a man. This woman was 100 per cent self-sufficient and empowered. She would tell Amanda to pick herself up, dust herself down, put some fucking lipstick on and get her shit together.

Yep, *her.*

Fuck you, Big.

CHAPTER 12

SAMANTHA

Worldwide web of men

As an escort, I get to meet men from all walks of life, all ages and stages, from all professions, from all states and countries. Here is my deduction so far on the lot of them – and, remember, this is only my opinion. If I've left your state/country out, it's only because either I haven't been there or haven't met anyone from there yet. (If you are an escort and completely disagree with me and have had different experiences than me, then that's your story. This is mine.)

Sydney: Sydney men are, on the whole, flaky and have average-sized dicks (I'll never get a client in Sydney again, will I?). They promise the earth but the only thing they deliver is either a few grams of cocaine and/or a whole lot of attitude and showy snobbery. For example, a man called Paul booked me for two hours, texted the day before to say he was looking forward to the date and then went AWOL. I was not surprised, nor had I planned for our date. I hadn't even shaved my legs as I knew he would be a typical Sydney time-waster.

Sydney is like an adult playground full of Peter Pans. The men never seem to grow up here. From what I've encountered, they fall into three categories: the businessman, the surfer and the gangster (the businessman and gangster have more in common than you'd think, except one wears a suit and is less honest).

I rarely work in Sydney; most of my clients are not from Sydney and I don't like seeing clients in Sydney – not because of the size of the penis but because it's my home town and it's where Amanda lives, not where Samantha works. But, saying that, I bend the rules for a few of my regulars, such as kinky lawyer Mark; Emerson, who manufactures health products; Mr Nice; a handsome banker called Jack, who has talented hands and good taste, and Richard, who plans his business trips from Perth to Sydney just so we can go for dinner. Oh! And Bill, and Steven the swimmer too. (I am paranoid about not mentioning all my clients. The ones who didn't make the cut in the first book would be extremely upset if they didn't make it into the second. If I've left you out, I apologise and will make it up to you in the bedroom.)

On the whole, Sydney clients (apart from my regs, of course) rarely dress well, even the wealthy ones, although what they do wear costs a lot of money. They can be unreliable, arrogant and smug. The best thing about them is that they rarely outstay their welcome, as they are always rushing off to some meeting or leaving early to miss the traffic. My Indian clients are always polite and reliable, even though they try to bargain. My Asian gentlemen are just that: gentlemen. The young Lebanese, on the whole, are very generous. They always pay in cash (big wads of it) and they rarely negotiate. I've never had a problem with them, even though they move in big groups, which can be intimidating, and they get loud and mouthy when all together. You definitely don't ask them what they do for work (it's always construction) but get them one on one and they are respectful and sweet, and very shy. Surprisingly so. And they never want that much sex. They would rather be seen *with* you than have sex, which is fine by me. I've had clients that I have seen one day, then a few months later I'll see their faces on the front page of the paper at some criminal's funeral. *Oh, there's so-and-so*, I'll think to myself, barely even raising an eyebrow that he's on the MOST WANTED list in Sydney. He was always so sweet ...

But the true blue Aussies? Put it this way: any issue or any time I have felt slightly uneasy or not quite sure about a client – or when, years ago, I was sexually assaulted in the Bordello – the cause has been a true blue Australian white-collar professional from Sydney.

Canberra: Despite its reputation for being full of weirdos (and that's just the politicians), I've not met one yet. It's not a cool, exciting city (is it even a city?) and some hotels I've stayed in could do with an overhaul (one in particular felt like a retirement home for fat Americans, especially at the buffet breakfast), but I thoroughly enjoy my clients in our great capital. They are lovely men, in a very simple, normal and endearing way: a bit like the super-smart kids at school who aren't the coolest. They know they don't live in a very dynamic place, but they are quick to boast that Canberra has some lovely parts to it (I asked where the CBD was once, only to be told that I was right bang in the middle of it). The men I see in Canberra dress sensibly and drive nice, sensible cars. They're not bad lovers, either, and I have had many an orgasm in a Canberra hotel room.

Canberra is a place where I have a lot of very wealthy

clients but, unlike Sydneysiders, they don't show their money off, and you certainly wouldn't know they had it from looking at them. I've had lovely dinners, visited amazing homes by the water, and been treated very well indeed.

One client – let's call him Bob – on our four-hour date even brings with him wine (alcoholic and non-alcoholic, because it's always a 10 a.m. date), crisps, dips and, wait for it, Freddo Frogs. Sometimes he jazzes it up a bit to surprise me and swaps the Frogs for a Caramello Koala. We talk politics, and don't get Bob started on religion. He scoffed at me once because I told him I believed in the afterlife. (Bob is worth millions, by the way, but dresses in ripped jeans and a checked shirt most of the time.)

Another client, Mal, who works in the public service, always asks if I want a lift from the airport to my hotel. 'It's no trouble, I'll come and pick you up,' he always gently insists. If truth be told, I'd prefer to take a taxi and get ready at the hotel alone, and I made the mistake of telling him that once. His silence was deafening. So every time I come to Canberra, Mal picks me up proudly in his freshly vacuumed BMW that smells of vanilla and chemical cleaning products, and drives me to my hotel, which takes less than eight minutes. He then waits in the car while I get ready and we drive to dinner. I think he enjoys the driving bit the most. After dinner, he jangles the keys just as I am shovelling the last bit of crème caramel into my mouth and says, 'Right, I'll get the car, shall I?'

I always make a mental note to remember to compliment him on his clean, shiny car, knowing that he cleans it just for me.

So that's Canberra men.

———————————

Brisbane: Forget it. Every escort has a lucky city and Brisbane isn't mine. Either I'm too expensive for them, too old, not blonde enough or just not their cup of tea. I've toured twice to Brisbane, and twice come back out of pocket. They either cancel or, even worse, just don't show up.

One client, an ex-army officer, booked me for three hours but when he turned up in his Rip Curl board shorts and tatty thongs, he confessed he only had enough money for half an hour. 'Come on, not even for me,' he whined with puppy-dog eyes as I showed him the door. I had to tell him simply and sharply that being good looking wasn't enough of a reason to get a freebie.

Mind you, I was bloody tempted: he was pretty hot, the only client in three days, and I was bored. But come on, Samantha, a girl has to stick to her principles.

Another man spent an hour on the phone telling me about his marriage split (she took the dogs!) and about his house on the water, and could I please do an overnight, and what kind of fish would I like for the BBQ (barramundi, please) he was going to cook for me ... only to cancel when I landed. *I'm sorry, the ex has taken all my money*, read the text.

This fair-haired bore still expected me to have hour-long conversations about his ex (who took the dogs and now his money!) and his house on the water. I have his name in my phone as 'Poor Time Waster No Dogs' now.

That trip I made a sulky promise as I waited for the flight at Brisbane airport, among the freckly men wearing short-sleeved work shirts, that I was never, ever going to tour Brisbane again.

Adelaide: Can't comment. Never been. But there's a lot of religious people there and some grisly murders (not that I am saying there is a direct correlation). I am sure it's a beautiful place, and if someone wanted to take me to the Barossa Valley for the weekend I would jump at the chance (if I carried out a police check on him first).

Melbourne: Ahhh, Melbourne. My Melbourne. The city of sophistication, handsome men and fantastic hotels. Every time the plane skids to a halt at Tullamarine airport, I know I'm in for a good time. The men tend to have big dicks, good haircuts, and enjoy lots of foreplay. The best sex I've had in my life has been in Melbourne (and the worst nights – and hangovers – I've had in my life have also been in Melbourne).

My clients in Melbourne are my favourites. Not only are they always so well dressed and well mannered, but they have something Sydney men lack (apart from size of manhood, class and manners, and a sense of style): I truly believe Melbourne men genuinely enjoy the company of women. They actually *like* women, as opposed to seeing them as a necessary evil. I've seen restaurateurs, office workers, students – from the age of eighty-four to twenty-one – and I cannot think of one negative about any of them – except maybe the 84-year-old ... I call it my little way of caring for the elderly community. It amazes me that 84-year-olds can still get it up, still ejaculate and still cheat on their wives. But, hey, who knows whether there are hookers in heaven, so he's probably cashing in.

People whinge about the weather in this city, but I am either in bed with a client or at one of the many fine eateries Melbourne has to offer. Everything is better there – including my sex life – so, yep, it's a big thumbs-up from me. I promised I would mention Ritchie and Dan from Melbourne, my sweet, cute, handsome young twenty-something clients; they both keep texting me telling me not to forget – so, hello, darling boys!

───────

Perth: What a jewel Perth is! What a delight! I was expecting another Brisbane if truth be told, with unreliable men in thongs and with no money, but not only did I make an awful lot of money on my first tour in Perth, I met some wonderful, interesting and intelligent men – mostly in the medical field (and not one rough-around-the-edges miner, sadly). The men who booked me in Perth booked me for minimum two hours, so they all had money, they were funny and kind, and all were mildly surprised when I told them how much I loved their city. The businessmen who congregate around St George's Terrace in the city have as much style and finesse as Melbournites, or men in any European city. They dress well, have good haircuts and good bone structure. Their penis size is ample and they are clean.

Clean is an important word, I've discovered, in Perth. Four of my Perth clients insisted on washing in our time together, either by having a long bath or a twenty-minute shower alone (truly) – even if our appointment was only for one hour. One even brought his own Body Shop bubble bath, with cinnamon to sprinkle on my you-know-what and a razor to shave me in the bath (even though I have been lasered). I also have a client who books me for one hour, showers for twenty minutes, then I have to shave his moustache to his chest hair, under his arms, then work the razor down to the forest of hair sprouting from his groin. Tiring, kind of gross and completely baffling as to why he pays $1100 for me to do this. He then jumps in the shower again for another twenty minutes.

'I think you've just come here for the shower and shave!' I yelled once, trying to make conversation through the steamed-up glass screen as the shower jets were on full blast.

'Yep, I do actually,' he shouted back as he merrily lathered his body.

Bloody expensive shower, I thought. Doesn't he have one at home? But oh, well … Nowt as queer as clients.

So that's Perth.

New Zealand: Every New Zealander I've met either looks like an ex-rugby player or like he's stepped out from the pages of a R.M. Williams catalogue. Kiwi men all have a brightness in their eyes, a sparkle. I've had a few Kiwi clients and can't fault them, except sometimes I can't understand what they say. M is my favourite: a manly, handsome farmer who lives opposite some picturesque lake with acres of land behind him, as do most New Zealanders. I love looking at photos of him on his tractor, with his dog, with his cows. I love him and always tell him so. Whether I mean I LOVE love him, I don't know, but I love being with him. His wife is a tall, striking blonde who has a figure I envy. They fight a lot, so he says. M and I always meet in the same spot, in the same hotel, and drink and eat the same food and have the same kind of sex, and that's been for three years now. Sex-wise it's never earth shattering with a Kiwi, but it's never anything unpleasant. Foreplay isn't a major thing for them but they make up for it in other ways, like cuddling you in bed with strong, hairy arms. Yum.

Americans: Escorts love a Yank. They're outgoing and warm, and they tip well. They love the fact that prostitution is not illegal here and so they're like kids in a candy shop. I often get phone calls from some American geriatric in Miami or Florida begging me to send girls there. I've seen a pastor from Texas, a guy who owned car parks, and a few American celebrities (that's a different chapter). They always have lots of money, they love Australians (I can't be bothered telling them I'm from London), and they tend to be good in bed. However, I've not met one who hasn't been overweight and they don't often stay in the nicest hotels, just the biggest ones. Penis wise: just like their tips – generous.

Europeans: Do Italians do it better? Yep (but they are the ones always in control). Spanish men are short, romantic and want you to dress up. Brazilians (not European, I know, but they speak Portuguese) want to try acrobatic positions and they like anal. The French are big on lingerie and seduction, plus they typically smoke and drink a lot of red wine in the bookings too.

English: My dear Brits, you make me laugh and we bond over Blighty, but typically British men are shy in bed and even more shy to ask for what they want. Sex is over quickly and I've yet to meet one who can do good dirty talk (stammering 'You're going to get a jolly good rogering when we get back to the hotel' doesn't do it for me). Penis size: generally above average. You won't be having a long time in bed, but it will be a fun time.

DISCLAIMER: Before I am inundated with complaints from men all over the world, please remember that this is just *my* experience. If you are a nice bloke from Brisbane who isn't out to waste my time, or a down-to-earth Sydneysider with a massive dick, great – but I haven't met you yet.

CHAPTER 13

AMANDA

Sex, lies, and Canberra

Apart from that night in the new fashionable Chinese restaurant when Big ordered the thin noodles, there wasn't a single point in time when I thought, *Right, I'm going back to work*. It just sort of happened.

All it took was a few emails from my regulars and instead of me fobbing them off with a 'sorry, can't do it for the next few weeks', I'd reply that yes, *of course* I can be at our usual hotel at 8 p.m. and *of course* I would love to stay a bit longer this time, and *yes, I've missed you too* ...

And you know what? I didn't feel one single bit of guilt.

Fuck you, Big. I'm not good enough for you? There are a million men out there who do *think I'm good enough.*

'Seriously, fuck him,' I'd snap to Tab tearfully. 'You're right, I'm never going to be part of his life. So he can sod right off.'

'So you've told him you're going back to work?'

'Er, no ...'

'You should tell him, Amanda. It's not fair that he's still giving you money.'

That was true, but I had made a decision that I wouldn't see new clients, just my regulars, like Mr Nice and Mark. So that didn't really count, did it? *Did it?*

It's not like I was putting myself out there again. The rumour in the industry was that I'd retired and I let people think that. But I was nervous about letting my regulars go for a man who had labelled me 'some girl in a bar' to his sister. In love I was; stupid I wasn't. Big didn't need to know – he wasn't giving me *that* much money, I told myself, and he would always make me ask for it, which you know I hated.

After that horrible night when he'd said it was going to take 'years' to be part of his life, well, that sealed it for me. As I had cried into scratchy serviettes, as Big had shaken his head at me, I had known Tab was right: nothing was ever going to change. And it's not a nice feeling to know that someone is ashamed of you. He wouldn't even put my real name in his phone – instead he called me 'Bill', so not to arouse interest if his kids or colleagues saw a call from Bill.

It wasn't easy, throughout this lying thing, and Big wasn't stupid either. Even though we lived in different states, he would call or text constantly: *Where are you? Who are you with? Take a photo. FaceTime me ...*

He was just as insecure as I was. I was jumpy, felt caged-in and watched. But that didn't stop me going back to work.

Remember how my counsellor, Doris, once told me to learn how to lie? Oh boy, I became an expert in deceit. You think men are the only ones to tell porkies? Nope. Women are better at it, we are smarter – and we rarely get caught. We mentally plan in advance, have a story made up – we even have photographic evidence to back it up. I know many escorts who lie to partners and boyfriends. I know many women who cheat on their husbands. Very, very rarely do I hear of them getting caught. But a bloke shags a woman who isn't his partner and not just his behaviour will give it away but little clues he will leave around. Receipts, phone bills, working out at the gym more, watching what he eats. If your sex life suddenly improves, I'd be suspicious, if I were you. He may be keen to put the new tricks he has learnt to work. I would be very surprised if a woman were caught like this.

I made sure I had a backlog of photos of my girlfriends and I having drinks, dinners and coffees, so when Big would ask for photos of what I was doing RIGHT NOW, I'd send him one I'd taken last week, and caption it *Dinner with the girls.*

You all look lovely. Love you, he'd text back.

Thanks. Miss you. Love you, I'd text nervously, before knocking on the door of an expensive hotel suite where a glass of cold Champagne and a client who was very happy to see me were waiting.

Ha! Not good enough? *Fuck you, Big.*

But it was hard work having a double life; how men seem to do it on a daily basis is beyond me. I was in a constant high alert of panic. I feel nervous just writing this, remembering the fear I lived with every day. Big would text or call every day, many times a day.

Who are you with? You're working, aren't you? What are you doing? Take a photo …

It didn't end.

That didn't stop me, though. *I'm still Bill in your contacts.* I'd show him not-good-enough.

Mark wanted to fly me to Canberra while he was on a conference: 'Just for the weekend, darling. We can go to the galleries and have dinner. I hear there's a fantastic show on … What time can you get here by?'

This would be a hard one. Big liked to FaceTime me every night at bedtime. It was his way of making sure I was alone and in my own bed. How would I get Big off my back this weekend? He was at some family wedding – of course, I wasn't invited – so that was Friday day and Friday night taken care of. But how would I swing it Saturday and Sunday?

'Yes, of course I'll come,' I told Mark. 'Book me on the next flight.'

Canberra was pleasant, as Canberra always is. I managed to avoid Big's texts for most of the weekend, until the Saturday afternoon.

Where have you been? What are you doing? Call me now please.

Shit. I'd used up my backlog of photos; I had nothing to give him. Mark and I were off to a gallery; he was humming as he was getting ready.

'I'll meet you out the front, I've got a few phone calls to make,' I told him.

I dashed out, my stomach in knots, dialling Big's number.

'Hi darling, so sorry, I've not been that well, I'm in bed, I've been sleeping most of the weekend,' I mumbled, covering my phone against the noises outside.

'Really? Take a photo, I want to see your pretty face,' he replied straightaway. Was he suspicious?

I quickly rubbed my make-up off, messed up my hair and did a quick zoom in on my face – and only my face.

I didn't airbrush it (as I usually did) to make sure I'd look wrinkly and pale, and *ping!* Send ...

'You look awful, get some rest,' he said, clearly studying my photo while talking.

'Yes, I'd better go.'

Just then, five roaring air force planes suddenly appeared out of nowhere, just above my head. Bloody Canberra. Bloody typical.

'Amanda? Are you there? What's that noise?'

'The washing machine! I'm standing by my washing machine! Shit, it's leaking everywhere ... better go ...' And I hung up, feeling like the world's most horrible person.

When Mark cheerily found me I was sitting on the steps to the hotel, biting off my acrylic nails.

'Oh, darling, whatever is the matter?' he said. 'Sorry, was I too long? I couldn't find my bloody glasses ...'

'No, it's not you, Mark,' I replied. 'It's me. Just problems at home. I'm fine. Sorry – let's go. I'm dying to see that latest collection by ...'

Texts and phone calls weren't Big's only tactics: he would invent a fake name and fake email address and send me an email to try to catch me out.

Hi Samantha, love to see you, heard a lot about you. Free for a dinner date next Tuesday?

He would sign it from Bob Smith or Jim Jones, hoping I wouldn't realise it was him and would fall into his trap. But I recognised his writing style and the words he used. And I wasn't taking on new clients. Every new enquiry I presumed was from him (and it usually was). I was in a constant state of super-awareness – and it was killing me.

Then the next time I saw Big, and he was on top of me, plunging his hardness deeper and deeper into me, I bit his shoulder, digging my nails into his back. Half pleasure, half pain. Why did I love this man? Why couldn't I stop working? Why couldn't I walk away from him? The situation was so toxic ... I was so bad ...

Thoughts would flood my head as his thrusts got harder and faster.

'I love you, Amanda,' he panted before he pulled out his cock and came all over my stomach.

'I love you too, Big,' I'd whisper, looking up at him. *I do love you, Big, I truly do. But it's never going to happen, is it? This is as good as it's going to get.*

And that was the way I justified working.

That was pretty much my life for the next six months or so. And I absolutely hated it.

CHAPTER 14

AMANDA

Four simple words

I am writing this chapter in the serene hinterland of my favourite Queensland retreat, eating a date slice and staring at the tropical rain as it therapeutically *tap-taps* the glass balcony doors while the shivering wallabies hop for cover.

I always joke that writing my books costs me a fortune. I need somewhere beautiful and quiet where I can lock myself away and write – and it always happens to be this same retreat, my chosen place of solitude.

I can spend hours in my suite writing, then join the rest of the guests at mealtimes, when we sit at big tables, wearing name tags, gently encouraged to socialise.

The question of work invariably comes up, and it did last night. And why shouldn't it, seeing as we spend 60 per cent of our lives working?

'So what do you do for work?' asked a very posh older lady who owned a mansion on the water in one of the most expensive streets in Sydney.

Eight sets of inquisitive female eyes suddenly started to blink at me.

I swallowed my mouthful of purple carrot and kale carefully, wondering what the hell to say.

Sod it: might as well tell them the truth.

'Oh me? Oh, I used to be a journalist for many years, before I split up with my ex, now I'm an escort and author, and I have my own escort agency ...'

The eyes kept blinking.

Then the posh lady put down her fork and rolled her eyes.

'Honestly, bloody journalists. You were good to get out of that industry, darling. I tell my mother not to believe everything she sees on Channel Nine and Seven, that she should watch the ABC instead, but she won't have a bar of it,' she said, shaking her head.

'Quite!' piped up another. 'The rubbish they write about these days, telling us who to vote for, what foods to eat, what gives you cancer ... Absolute rubbish! They think we're idiots. I don't buy newspapers anymore, apart from to read my horoscope.'

Then an elderly lady, her white hair tied very neatly in a bun, touched my hand.

'Amanda, good for you, darling,' she said. 'Much more ethical job, isn't it, what you do now. Aren't you glad you're not in the media anymore? Tell us what it was like working for the press. Tell me – I'm sure you get this all the time – have you met Piers Morgan? And what's happening with Karl Stefanovic's marriage? His poor wife … I never liked that man.'

So it went on. These very posh ladies from all over Australia were more interested in which celebrities I'd met, and what it was like working under ferocious editors, than in getting hot and bothered about me being a sex worker. I was almost disappointed.

Once word got round the retreat that there was an author/escort among us, a few women were keen to know more, thirsty for snippets of gold about what I'd learnt about men, or where they could buy my book, or else they'd thought of a business idea for me. One even said – while we were lying in the relaxation room, on big, fluffy cushions in our fluffy white dressing gowns – that she knew who I was the minute I sat down for dinner.

'Oh yes, I've been following your story in the press,' she said with a smile, sipping her watery herbal tea. 'Loved your book!'

Mostly they just wanted to say bloody well done – their husbands had left them for the secretary and if they could do what I do, they would – *so, good for you, girl.*

'I think you're marvellous,' said one very rich blonde divorcée from Sydney's exclusive Point Piper. Her husband had been bonking his junior work colleague in their marital bed. She'd caught him by watching their CCTV surveillance, after the maid had tipped her off. 'When we get out of this place and my bloody renovations are finished, you're coming to mine for a Champagne.' (By the way, we have met since our retreat and I am lucky enough to call her and her gorgeous partner friends.)

I have to say, it's nice to be accepted by my own kind. Most women just get it – they really do.

But I know I'm one of the lucky ones.

I know that doesn't happen for all other escorts, and I know there are many women out there petrified that their cover will be blown and the whole world will know they are a sex worker and their life will be in ruins.

My life didn't end up that way. Look, I'm not saying I don't get gossiped about; I'm sure I do. I'm sure people quietly judge me, as we all do with everyone. But my fellow females, I have to say, have been fantastic. Women who I thought would look down their noses at me or exclude me from their lives or their dinner parties, or not want me in their homes or minding their kids – well, that simply hasn't happened.

Just the other week, I was in my local bank. I had a huge wad of cash that I wanted to deposit.

'Look, I'm sorry, I have no idea how much is there – would you mind counting it for me?' I asked the middle-aged lady behind the counter, who, according to her name tag, was called Janelle and was a Senior Bank Consultant.

'No problem,' she replied, thumbing quickly and efficiently through the thousands.

When she passed $11 000, and still counting, she raised an eyebrow – but still kept counting.

'I'm not a drug dealer,' I smiled at her, moving closer to the glass screen. 'I'm an escort.'

'Oh wow, really?' She turned to face me, her eyes lighting up.

'Yes, this is the money I made in Perth recently. I put it in the bank, I pay my taxes ...'

'I don't make this much in a few months!' She came in closer to whisper. 'I've been thinking about a career change. I'm a single mother and I never see my teenage daughter. Do you think I could do it? Am I pretty enough? Can we have a coffee next week?' I very subtly slid a business card under the glass window. She beamed and slipped it quickly into her bag.

Another time I found myself sitting on an orange plastic chair in the rooms of a new doctor I hadn't seen before: Dr Desiree Johnson, a beautiful redhead who was in her late fifties and still exuded class, grace and beauty.

'I may as well have all my tests done too, now that I'm here,' I said.

'Right ... but I'm just looking at your records, Amanda – you had them done three months ago?' She peered at me from under her spectacles.

'Yes, but I'm a sex worker and get tested regularly,' I explained.

She looked at me with a smile, then took her glasses off.

'Are you really? Isn't that wonderful. I envy you. Did you know, ever since that bastard ex-husband of mine pissed off with my neighbour, I've fantasised about escorting. I'm a doctor – I prod enough bodies I don't really want to prod. But, as you know, it's just a job. I don't see what the big deal is, I can disconnect. I'm sick of these long hours. Do you have a business card?'

And I'm not going to say much about my Angels, to protect their identity, but I will say that I have lawyers, doctors and business owners, to name but a few, on my books.

I've had women who have been abused by their husbands and left with nothing. I've had women who do this on the side with their husbands' blessing. I've had an Angel who lost 40 kilograms and wanted to celebrate her sexiness by empowering herself (also with her husband's blessing). She runs a high-powered business with forty staff.

I've had women who are sick to death of dating and want to be the one in control for a change. I've had women in their fifties and sixties work for me – one a grandmother with five grandkids!

It takes all sorts; all women from all walks of life. Some come to me worrying about how they're going to pay their kids' school fees, and saying they've lost their power and confidence. It's nice to see them a few months later, with a few clients under their belt and a bank account full of a few thousand dollars they didn't have before. They walk a bit taller, a bit prouder. Their spark comes back. One of my Angels, a 44-year-old well-spoken mother whose husband left her with nothing, called me after a dinner date with a client.

'It is so nice being able to sleep at night now knowing I can pay the rent,' she said.

There are millions of sex workers all around the world, each with their unique personal story. Some do it because they love it; some do it because they have to; some, sadly, do it because they have no choice.

Who is anyone else to judge what these women do with their lives and bodies? I came out guns blazing publicly on TV and I wear my decision no matter what happens, good or bad. I owned it – and then where can people go with it? If you own something and admit it, you take the sting out: *Yes, I had an affair. Yes, I lied. Yes, I am an escort.* By owning something and being honest about it, you take away someone else's power over you. I know girls who tell me that clients threaten to expose them, or other sex workers *do* expose them. But if you own it, they can't blackmail you.

No one has got anything on me. One of my Angels' ex-partners threatened to report me to the tax office when he found out she was working for me. Go for it! They owe *me* money! And that, to me, is power: when you are upfront and honest – own it so no one else can.

That isn't everyone's choice. I get that we all have unique situations. We all have our own story, whatever our profession. But as a woman, only you can decide what you do with your body. *Only you.*

There's one thing I drum into the minds of my Angels and the women I mentor, made up of four very simple words.

Your body, your choice.

No one has the right to judge you or tell you what to do with your own body, especially not a man.

Your body, your choice.

Remember that.

Okay?

CHAPTER 15

SAMANTHA

Celebrity clients

I know what you're thinking – I must get to have sex with all sorts of celebrities. Handsome actors, male models, famous sportsmen! Lucky old me, eh? An old duck like me getting my long talons on a variety of perfect, delicious bodies …

Think again.

————————

Sportsmen: It depends on the sport but, mostly, young, handsome men who are famous for playing some sort of game that involves a ball are a pain in the backside. They CANNOT BELIEVE you still want to charge them, because they are so handsome and famous, and every single woman is out there chasing them! I've had sportsmen who've had beautiful wives and model fiancées knock on my door – so to speak – and I hear the same story. Quite often the marriage is for their image and publicity, and, quite clearly, there isn't much love involved. I do have one favourite sportsman, however – who, of course, I won't name but he is a true gentleman in every sense of the word.

Tennis players tend to be very nice, although a bit dull, and there isn't much conversation. Swimmers are fit and, again, very polite, but I wouldn't be surprised if they are all members of Hillsong. They have this too-healthy inane glint in their eyes, and shiny skin that, frankly, isn't natural. It's either chlorine or Jesus Christ doing it.

Golfers are quite meticulous, and I haven't met one yet who hasn't worn a polo shirt and had terrible sun damage. AFL: long and lean. NRL: built like stallions. Forget rugby union being a gentleman's game – both league and union men are sweet and polite. League tend to be family men (except when they're with me), and they all love their mums.

I remember I had one gorgeous Olympian who was visiting from the UK – my god, he was stunning. But he couldn't handle the guilt and spent an hour afterwards showing me photos of his beautiful wife.

The plus side to sportsmen: their backs! Have you ever

run your fingers down a toned, fit back? Their shoulder blades ... *Dreamy*.

The downside: their arrogance. 'Do you know how much I earn?' (No, but clearly it can't be much, as you still expect free sex.) They also fuck like a jackhammer. Being pumped hard and thrown around the room like a footy ball may be impressive on the field, lads, but when you are with a lady, try to exercise some control. We are women, not blow-up dolls (even though we may try to look like one).

TV stars: TV people are completely paranoid about being caught. Maybe it's all the drugs they do, or the fact that they might be in the papers and their wives will take them to the cleaners, but on the whole, men who work in TV behind the scenes and on-screen would rather report *on* the news than *be* the news. They all hate each other and would do anything to dob the other team in. The young, handsome ones who have just got a break or a spot on some soap opera are an absolute pain in the backside. But I do what I do if I see them on the telly: simply sit there and switch off.

And here's one thing I will say, and have always said: the bigger the celebrity, the more professional they are – apart from the one I am going to tell you about.

A very, very famous A-list celebrity books my Angels every time he is in Australia. He is worth, I would estimate, $100 million at least. And he *negotiates* on the price of my girls. Yup. He bargains me down. Instead of paying $800, he pays $600 (that's Australian dollars). He doesn't bargain me down on the phone (or, rather, his manager doesn't) – he waits until I am sitting in front of him enjoying a nice glass of Champagne (as we all watch him swigging from his own bottle of Moët – and I had to fetch my drink myself). Fascinating fact: he also had the hotel bring up a microwave, so he could reheat his McDonald's. Anyway, his manager whispered in my ear that so-and-so wasn't going to pay the full fee and could we do something with the price? I was so angry I went to the bathroom, sat on the heated toilet seat and contemplated stealing the soap and selling it on eBay. I knew the right thing was to say no, but my two Angels sitting out there were so excited to be in his company that I went back and agreed. I took the financial hit; the girls didn't lose any money. Instead, hearing what the girls said about him in the bedroom was entertaining enough.

I do have a story about a certain Hollywood celebrity – but he had no idea I was an escort. I was having dinner in a local restaurant when he turned up with his entourage. Before he ordered dessert, he also ordered me and my girlfriend to come and sit with him – which, of course, we did. How exciting! So-and-so wanted our company! He seemed nice enough, and when he asked to come back to my house for a 'cup of herbal tea', I thought, *Why not?* – maybe that was code for sex, drugs, and rock 'n' roll with a handsome A-lister.

It wasn't.

As soon as he walked in, he plonked himself down with his boots up on my sofa. He asked me to make him a herbal tea, then asked if I had any painkillers (his drug of choice) and started quoting lines from his movies. I kid you not. My crush on him dissolved faster that the green tea in the teacup. I could not believe what a cliché he was.

'Take your top off,' he demanded, smiling.

'Um … *you* take *your* top off, then I will …'

So he paraded around my living room with no T-shirt (okay, he had a great body).

'Now you do it,' he said.

'Sorry, no, and while you're up can you take your shoes off?'

Bored of hearing how great he was in such-and-such movie, and had I seen him in that movie (no), I asked him to leave.

'Sorry, darling, I'm getting the kids back tomorrow and I want to go to bed,' I said.

'Oh? You don't want company?'

'No, thanks.'

'Why don't you come back to mine and we can snuggle all night?'

'Thanks, but no.' (*I'd rather stick hot needles in my eyes.*)

A few days later, I started to regret it. Maybe I should have shagged him – just for the hell of it. I mean, I've shagged a man with a plastic ear, for god's sake – why couldn't I do it with a handsome Hollywood actor? The reason was, quite simply, that he was a dickhead. Even if money had been involved, I would have struggled. I may be an escort and sell my time, but I am the one making the choice as to who my body goes to for an hour or two. Give me the man with the plastic ear any day. Deformities I can deal with; dickheads I can't.

Pop stars: Actually, I can't comment as I have never had a pop-star client. At least, I can't remember if I have. But I know one escort who has, and she said they drank herbal tea all night. What is it with bloody herbal tea? They don't even drink the hard stuff, like English Breakfast! No sex, no drugs, no rock 'n' roll. How boring!

CHAPTER 16

AMANDA

Clients who counsel

The tears came thick and fast.

'Big is such an arsehole,' I panted, trying to get the words out through my tears. 'He's blocked me because of my latest post on Twitter, but I keep telling him I have to do it and now he's not talking to me.'

'Amanda, this guy is a dickhead; an absolute tool. I don't know why you stay with him. You can do so much better ... I hate hearing you cry. Do you want me to sort him out?'

Nope, this wasn't Tab – it was Joe, one of my clients from Melbourne. An Italian–Aussie businessman who I have been seeing for years. I call him Joe Bananas, when clearly that isn't his name, and he calls me Amanda, because when you've been seeing a client as long as I've been seeing Bananas, it feels weird when he calls me Samantha. Mind you, it feels a bit weird sometimes calling a grown man Bananas – but after all these years I still don't know what his name is, nor where he works. His email address is Joe Bananas and he uses a secret phone. All I know is that he is in his late forties, is a well-known banker in the CBD, wears nice suits, has a family he adores, probably has connections in the Mafia ('No comment' he says, smiling, when I ask) and likes me to wear latex (that's the only annoying bit). He sees me for one hour, never longer, every time I tour Melbourne and sex is always doggie style, hard and fast. He always leaves my $1000 hidden behind the taps in the bathroom (I think he likes doing it that way as it removes the 'business' side of things).

Joe and I have become close. Often our hour would be spent with fifteen minutes foreplay and sex, and forty-five minutes talking – usually about me and my life. And Big.

And when Big and I fought, as we always did, I would often call Joe in tears. And, of course, Joe being my client, and Italian, would always take my side and be fiercely protective. Just the way I liked it. And he would say things like this every time I called him up crying …

'Send him a fish wrapped in newspaper. That will give him a message Mafia style.'

'Don't you mean a horse's head in the bed?'

'No, Amanda. If he is a real man, he will know the meaning of a fish in newspaper.'

Or: 'Tell him "Mal Occhio" from me.'

'Mal what?'

'Malocchio. If this prick is as Catholic as he says he is, he'll know what that means.'

So I'd say all these things to Big, like 'Malocchio,' or I'd tell him I was going to send him a fish wrapped in newspaper if he wasn't careful, and Big would just laugh.

'Who the fuck is telling you all this crap?' he said once. 'Al Bloody Pacino?'

But our fights continued, this battle for power, and my confidence eroded. I still saw clients, but my heart wasn't in it.

I shouldn't be doing it, it's bad, escorting is bad, lying is bad, taking his money is bad, I am bad. Repeat after me: I am bad.

Once, a long time ago now, Samantha would be quaffing Champagne, touching my client's knee, laughing at his jokes. Now I was nervously checking my phone every two minutes, hoping my client would go to the bathroom so I could text Big, the pained look of guilt all over my face.

I called M the handsome Kiwi once when I was drunk late at night.

'I hate Big so much, he keeps blocking me,' I snorted through tears 'He's never going to let me meet his family, is he? Do you think he will? Would you ever date an escort? Am I that bad a person?'

'What the hell are you doing with this man?' he replied in his thick New Zealand accent. 'He sounds like a bloody idiot. He knew what you were when he met you. No, you're not going to meet his family, darlin', and yes, if I wasn't married to the bloody bitch from hell I'd marry you.'

Then he stayed on the phone as I howled even more. But it didn't seem to bother him: he still booked me every time he came to Sydney.

'And please tell me you've got rid of that man?' he would ask each time, popping another lukewarm arancini ball into his mouth at our usual hotel bar (same food, same bar, remember?).

'Oh, him? Yes, long gone,' I'd lie, not wanting to talk about it; not wanting my issues to take over his precious time. 'Thank you for being so sweet. Wow, have you been to the gym? You look so fit. And new shoes!'

Mark the lawyer was just as concerned.

'Darling, you seemed so sad when I saw you last night,' he said, calling me the next day to see if I was okay.

'Was I? I'm sorry, Mark,' *Shit.* I couldn't lose Mark, he was one of my most loyal. I had to be on my best behaviour. *Come on, Amanda. He's not paying you to look miserable. Sharpen up. Pull yourself together.*

'I promise I'll be better next time I see you ...'

'Don't apologise, darling! I'm just worried about you. You're always so kind to me, you always help me when I am feeling down, and I want you to know I am here for you.'

See, I told you my clients were nice, didn't I?

So I'd tell Mark about Big, and ask him if he would ever date an escort and would he make the escort give up work, and *blah blah.* And the response from him – and all my other poor clients that I bored to tears with my relationship woes – was the same: 'Darling, Big should love you for who you are. You are a special woman, one of a kind. You give up working when you want to, not when someone else tells you to.'

Followed closely by: 'But you'll still see me, right?'

CHAPTER 17

SAMANTHA

Professor Peter Pan

With absolute horror, I've just realised that I haven't written about Professor Peter Pan. He would be absolutely devastated if I didn't dedicate one whole chapter to him. And he deserves a bit of dedication, seeing as he dedicates his life to saving our planet.

Professor Peter Pan is a neat, trim married man in his fifties who quite literally saves the world for a living. An academic with a zillion degrees in Saving Our World, he says things like: 'Tell your children not to have children' and 'If things carry on the way they are, we've got about seventy years left on this planet.'

I probably only see him twice a year because he is always buried nose deep in some eco project in Zambia or marching up some mountain in Peru, or heading up some voyage to some faraway country where he studies icebergs, ecosystems or grains of sand. And he always comes back with bad news.

'It's not looking good, Samantha,' he always says, shaking his head, when I ask. 'So we may as well have as much fun as we can!'

On our first date, after I'd signed his copy of *Hooked* (he was an avid fan, he confessed), he went to the freezer to retrieve my gift. He had just come back from a world-saving expedition to Antarctica, or the North Pole – I can never remember.

'I brought this all the way back from my trip!' he beamed, opening the freezer door.

Oh goodie, vodka! I thought, licking my lips.

He took out an ice tray and proudly placed it on the table in front of me. I stared at it. Ice? Aha! Ice for the bottle of vodka he is now going to bring out ...

'Water! Frozen water from a real iceberg! I carried this all the way from Antarctica, through Customs, just for you, Samantha! And it hasn't melted a bit!'

Okay, it wasn't alcoholic, but still ... How could you not be touched by such generosity? I was extremely humbled. (It melted by the time I got home and I had to use an old beach towel to wipe it off my car seats, but I've never told him that.)

Professor Peter Pan is also very honest. 'You are not the best sex I've ever had, Samantha,' he said smartly once, after ejaculating.

'Oh really?' I replied while easing the condom off his still-throbbing cock.

'Yes, really ...' And he would rattle off a few names of escorts who did anal and would squirt (no doubt at the same time) and perform all sorts of magic tricks, before he said quietly, 'But you are the one I am in love with.'

'Oh shut up.' I nudged him, laughing. 'You're not in love with me, you psychopath. Are you? Oh for god's sake, Peter – you're not, are you?'

His silence spoke a thousand words as he turned to face the other way. Oh dear. He was.

'Well, you know I love you in a non-weird way, don't you?' I said, cuddling close to him, wrapping my arms around his slim, fit body. 'My Professor Peter Pan who saves the planet.'

I was surprised: Professor Peter Pan is a highly intelligent man. And a man who sees other escorts (who are much better in bed than me). He should know the rules. Since when do love and sex belong in the same sentence in this game?

One morning, after an overnight together in Sydney – and after he had ejaculated in not one but *two* ribbed condoms – he sat down by my side of the bed with a solemn look on his academic face.

'Samantha, I cannot see you anymore,' he said seriously. 'This is torture for me. Absolute torture. I am in love with you and it kills me. I feel depressed every time you walk out of that hotel door. I cannot stand it. I cannot concentrate on work. I cannot save this planet after I see you. Tell me, am I a fool? Do you think of me all the time too?'

'Um, yes, but ...'

'I cannot bear it. It is torture. Torture. I am suffering. My work is suffering, Samantha. I've got to give a talk today on the worrying changing mating habits of bumble bees and all I can think of is your wet pussy in my face.'

'Oh dear, Peter – I don't want to be responsible for the decline of the planet ...'

'Come on, be serious for once. You don't think of me, do you? Do you think of me when you leave this hotel room?'

'Um, I do.'

'You don't! I am torturing myself by seeing you. No more, Samantha. This is the last time you will ever see me. I have decided. The last time.' And then he got up and buttoned his shirt in dramatic silence as I sat in bed, drinking my coffee, watching him.

Don't worry. Don't feel too sorry for Professor Peter Pan. Don't think I've lost him.

We have this conversation every bloody time we see each other (actually, he has this conversation to himself out loud in front of me, and I listen intently, trying not to smile). I don't want him leaving his wife, his family for Samantha! Samantha has her own life.

I don't know what gets into the heads of these men sometimes. One client told me once, 'If my wife and I ever split up, don't worry, Sam, I'm going to marry you,' as he tapped my bum, giving me a comforting wink.

I smiled weakly. Should I fall to my knees, my hands clasped together, praising the Lord that a 65-year-old retiree with gout, who farted every time I went down to suck his feeble cock, wanted to marry me?

What on earth do these men think? Either I am doing my job too well or they are completely delusional. Possibly both.

That doesn't mean I'm not extremely fond of Peter – or any of my clients in a special way. I am. While I don't want to marry them, or even date them, I think of them often and appreciate their uniqueness.

And I know he thinks about me a lot. Every country he visits, I get a little gift. He buys me brightly coloured scarfs from Spain, my very rare and special perfume from Paris

(I'm not telling which one because then you'll all buy it and it won't be special anymore), shoes from Italy. He recently sent flowers to wish 'us' a Happy Anniversary.

> *It has been two years since we met. I love you, my little Tinkerbell. Love Professor Peter Pan, your favourite Psycho.*

CHAPTER 18

AMANDA

The obligatory taxi driver story

For those who thumbed through the pages of *Hooked*, you'd remember the female taxi driver who, through my tears, made me repeat 'Garbage in, garbage out'.

Well, this is another one of those taxi driver stories (every book has to have at least one).

I'd just picked up this speeding Silver Service automobile outside one of my favourite hotels in Sydney, my sunglasses once again masking my red, worried eyes and dark circles.

I had just done an overnight with kind but kinky lawyer Mark, and when I am with him, I am 99 per cent present. Or I try to be.

But it had been fourteen hours of Big texting and calling, and the more time that passed between me answering the messages, the more controlling and abusive they got.

Where are you? What are you doing?

Then:

If you don't respond, I'm calling the police.

To:

You're a bitch ... You're clearly doing something with someone you shouldn't be ...

And so it went on. I sat with Mark through drinks while my phone was vibrating, I sat with Mark through dinner while my phone was vibrating, and as I whispered in his ear how I wanted to get fucked by another cock while he was watching, my phone was vibrating.

'Everything okay, darling?' Mark remarked as I leaned over to check my phone. Twenty-one messages.

'Just setting the alarm,' I replied feebly, my stomach in knots. I couldn't cope with the pressure, the stress. *I am such a bad person, I am such a bad person. What am I doing here? I should be with Big ...*

Those thoughts swirled and swirled around in my head constantly. And when morning came, and I sat with Mark for our coffee, my phone was vibrating. I waited, through gritted teeth, for Mark to finally peck me on the cheek and walk the 10 minutes to his office, then I hailed a taxi in a panic and read Big's last message, wondering what the fuck my excuse should be this time.

Don't bother calling me back. You're dumped. Blocking you. Forget any more money from me. You're on your own now.

I threw my phone down on the leather car seat and let the tears fall. How long could I do this? How long could I keep trying to make everyone happy? My clients, Big, me?

Tab kept telling me that this relationship would give me cancer with all the crying I did, and I had started to believe her.

'Here,' piped up the taxi driver with an Indian accent. 'I have tissues.' And without taking his eyes off the road, he passed me a big box of Kleenex from the front passenger seat.

'Oh, thank you,' I replied, blowing my nose, barely glancing up. 'That's sweet, thanks.'

So what was I going to do? It wasn't fair to mess Big around, but could I really give up work for him? Would I ever be more than 'some girl in a bar'? Could I trust and believe that one day I would be good enough to be part of his life?

I couldn't cope with the pressure any more. I couldn't cope with his constant doubt, his constant messages, his constant threats. He wanted commitment? What commitment had he shown me – apart from sex on tap for him and a companion for nice dinners. Once again the tears fell and the tissue got darker and darker with my salty water.

'Excuse me, miss,' the driver piped up again. 'I am sorry to ask, but what is the matter? You can tell me it is none of my bloody business but you are sad and I do not like seeing anyone sad in my taxi.'

'Oh, you're very sweet – it's just man problems,' I replied, blowing my nose. 'You know how it is.'

'Oh yes, yes, indeed,' he replied, smiling, shaking and nodding his head all at the same time. 'Oh dearie me, I have got this all to come.'

'Oh?' I asked, intrigued.

He laughed. 'I am transitioning. I am becoming a woman. I no longer want to be a man. I don't even like men very much.'

I pulled the tissue away from my nose. I couldn't have heard right: this man was big and muscly. He even had a beard. He was undoubtedly a man. A man's man.

'You're what? Sorry, I don't think I heard that correctly.'

'I am becoming a woman,' he said. 'I am already on hormone treatment. I am driving taxis to pay for my breasts that I shall get in Thailand. The doctors there will also operate on me, down there ... I have always felt like a woman. Even though I used to play cricket back home in India, even my family knew. I was born in the wrong body. So I understand. I understand why you are crying. Men are not nice. They are not nice at all.'

I swear to god my angels put me in these situations when they know I need some light entertainment. 'Take her mind off things,' they probably chimed from their clouds. 'Send her a little distraction.'

As we sped past the clattery cafes of Darlinghurst and the expensive boutiques of Paddington, and right to the second he stopped outside my little beachside home, I was hooked on his every word.

'So you have a good day, miss,' he said, turning around to give me my change. 'Do not cry over a man again. They are not worth it.'

'Thank you, you've absolutely taken my mind off things,' I replied, lighter, smiling now as I opened the door. 'Good luck with your operation – and sorry, I didn't even ask your name.'

He looked at me with a twinkle in his chocolate brown eyes. 'My real name is Sam, but you can call me Samantha.'

CHAPTER 19

SAMANTHA

Most people are nice

There are a few nasty women in the sex industry.

There are a few nasty women whichever industry you work in. I remember being bullied at the TV station I worked at by a certain female colleague who, quite literally, would stamp her high-heeled feet and hiss in my ear that I was to report to her and her only (I wasn't meant to, actually). And then she demanded to know just how long I would be working there (presumably because she didn't want me around).

'What is it, Amanda – days, weeks, *months*?' she would snarl, her heavily caked-on face so close to mine that her spit landed on my chin.

In my experience as Samantha I have encountered a few nasty women – other sex workers – as well. I'm not the only escort to suffer at the hands of bitchy bullies and I won't be the last. And I would urge any woman in this industry who is being bullied by one of their own to hang out with me and my escort friends instead – we have a zero tolerance policy on nastiness.

It would appear, though, that any sex worker is considered fair game for this lot. I've had girls calling me, upset at being blacklisted from their escort pages, where other sex workers share news and support, and report dodgy clients. It would appear if the founder of the page doesn't like you, she won't let you join, so not only are you on the outer (even though you've never met these women), you are not privy to vital information about clients that could save your life. I've had women confide in me that they've had to block so-and-so escort because she kept stealing ideas and clients. I know women whose real names were outed on social media by jealous sex workers.

It's never to our faces, of course – that would take balls. It doesn't even take place over the phone in a one-to-one conversation. It happens online, on Twitter, on Facebook, on email – someplace where they are the invisible masters of their own ramblings and vitriol.

The thing that triggered it in my case? Whenever something I wrote was published in the mainstream press, regardless of the topic (don't get them started on the pink nail polish debacle – google it). Any time I had an opinion piece in the papers, the nastiness would go into overdrive.

'Who the fuck does Samantha X think she is?'

'Why doesn't she shut up, no one wants to hear her pathetic drivel.'

'How dare she tell us what to do.'

'I heard she's not really an escort and made the whole thing up.'

'She's an embarrassment to the sex industry.'

'She really rates herself ... She's such a moron ...'

'She's only doing it to promote her business.'

'All my clients think she's awful. They would never see her ...'

'I had a client that thinks she's not all that.'

'And she's not even that pretty!'

'We hate Samantha X.'

'Yeah, we hate Samantha X!'

And so it went on. Comments written by sex workers about another sex worker. Lovely bunch, eh! Just imagine what a bundle of joy they are with their clients!

To be honest, I don't read it. I never do – I'm a firm believer that sometimes ignorance is bliss. I only know what's been written because a few of the nice ones (and there are more nice than not) call me up to tell me.

'Honestly, Samantha, don't read it,' one escort told me. 'These women are absolutely appalling and an embarrassment to our industry.'

A few who I had never spoken to or met contacted me out of the blue to tell me that they were sorry for the nastiness and that I had their support, which was extremely touching.

'I was on the receiving end last year, so I know exactly how you are feeling,' one said.

'While I don't always agree with you, Samantha, I respect you as a woman, and no one should be spoken about like that,' said another.

The support from women I had never met was humbling.

But fuck the bullies, seriously. What was it, jealousy? Anger that because I wasn't picketing outside Parliament House in ripped stockings and smudged red lipstick that I didn't care about sex workers' rights? I should be suffering! We all should be suffering! Politicians will only listen when we show them we are angry!

Did they think I was doing a disservice to escorts by writing about the industry, about *my* experience?

Did these women not think, for one moment, that to be a crusader of the sex industry doesn't always mean you need to get angry and march in some rally, waving a board that says: *MY PUSSY HAS POWER!!* written in their period blood?

We each have our own way.

And I had my own way.

I outed myself on TV and wrote a book about how I believed the sex industry can be a powerful industry for women, how I enjoyed my role as an escort a great deal and the job wasn't always about sex.

That as a former journalist I found escorting far more empowering, and the women I'd met so far in the industry were smart, sane and doing it for the right reasons.

That the clients I met were not rapists and weirdos but normal men with normal desires.

Sure, I partly did it for book sales – of course I did. I'd just written my memoir; I'm a businesswoman. Who wouldn't want to promote their book on national TV, given the chance?

But did they think that was an easy thing to do?

Because of it, my parents and I are estranged, and I have to live with my decision for the rest of my life.

I'll always be 'that woman'.

Did they think that was easy?

Didn't these women understand that by having mainstream media sit up and listen to one of their own, I was trying to, in my very small way, help destigmatise an industry in which women – including them and me – are forever demonised?

It's not a big part I play, but seeing my name in the newspapers gives me a thrill. Not because I've got my name in the papers and it means it's good for business and I get recognised in the street – but because slowly, surely, Australia is becoming more accepting of sex workers and the industry we work in. People can no longer pretend we don't exist, and their perception that we are clearly mad, crazy junkies being forced to turn tricks to feed our habits is slowly dying.

If the daily newspapers care – and publish – what escorts think, that means they know there are people who want to read it. Yes, I am controversial; yes, I say things that get people's backs up; yes, my website gets a surge when I am in print. But, more important than that, a sex worker is being given a voice. Some stressed-out editor somewhere in some news meeting says, 'Yes, let's publish what a sex worker thinks about this issue.' And that is only a good thing, isn't it?

I admit, I'm not much interested in politics. Test me on the ridiculous laws in every state and I'll trip up. I'm happy to leave that to the experts in the sex industry, and the wonderful work of organisations like SWOP (Sex Workers

Outreach Program). They work extremely hard to make sure sex workers stay safe, that our rights are heard and our laws fair.

That's what they do. And they do it well.

Let me do what *I* do.

So, sure, you may not like what I say; you may not agree. I don't expect people to agree. But what I don't expect is women who are supposed to be on the same team pulling, scratching and tearing each other down.

This job is hard enough, and we face enough backlash from the public that we don't need to start attacking each other. It's immature, it's nasty and it is the behaviour of a schoolyard bully. And no one likes a bully.

CHAPTER 20

AMANDA

Busted

It was never going to last, this web of deceit I'd weaved. It has been said that the truth always comes out in the end – and it did for me one evening when I was out with girlfriends and Big decided to stay at mine to catch up on some work.

'You go, darling, I've got so much to do,' he said, dropping me off at the restaurant. 'You don't mind, do you? Say hi to the girls ...'

Just when I had finished my second glass of chardonnay, the text message from Big came. I felt my phone vibrate, saw Big's name and rolled my eyes. He'd just dropped me off – what had I done wrong now?

Except it wasn't words. It was a photograph. It was a photograph he'd taken of one of my emails from my laptop.

'Eh?' I thought, zooming in, trying to read the tiny black words.

Oh fuck. Fuckety fuck.

It was a photograph of an email Mr Nice had sent me thanking me for a great night. Last week.

More messages pinged through. More photographs of emails from clients.

From Mark: *Darling, did you want to try a new hotel this time? I feel we've done the usual place so many times …*

And: *Hey Samantha, great to see you in Melbourne. Let me know when you're next down. Cheers, Dan.*

And: *Hey stranger, I'm doing a sneaky visit to Canberra next week. Will you be around? No pressure, just love to see you, Samantha XXX*

Big had been snooping on my laptop. And he'd found the evidence he was looking for. You always do when you look for it, and there it was in black and white. Samantha was back working – or had she ever stopped?

It's okay. I'm not angry, were his eerily calm words. The silent assassin.

I was even more scared.

Two glasses of chardonnay turned into six, turned into cocktails turned into me vomiting in a toilet in a club in Double Bay, too scared to go back to my own house. Would my laptop be smashed on the floor? Would he be gone, taking all my gifts back too? Would my dogs have their throats slit?

As 2 a.m. rolled around I quietly unlocked my front door, and tiptoed over a snoring Rosie into my bedroom, my stomach in sickly knots at what I would find.

Big was sitting up in bed reading papers on the stock markets, drinking a cup of tea. When he saw me come in he put his papers down on my bedside table and looked at me, his face expressionless.

'Well, that's that then, isn't it, Amanda?' he said calmly.

I bowed my head in shame as the drunk tears rolled onto the carpet, with all sorts of thoughts swimming around in my head. But the only thing I remember thinking was: *Who the fuck is going to be my NOK now?*

CHAPTER 21

SAMANTHA

The (un)lucky accountant from Albury Wodonga

Usually when a group of girls get together, things get messy. When a group of escorts get together, things get even messier. The place was a plush hotel in Sydney, the time was early evening and the escorts were myself and three other women: Star, a short peroxide blonde with a degree in law (well, she says that but she actually dropped out in term two), Sarah, an elegant, tall mother of three who grew up with fiercely religious parents, and Ness, a big-boobed brunette who was a bit too partial to lip fillers.

There wasn't an occasion – we never needed an occasion. It was a catch-up, an afternoon coffee to see how we were all going and to bitch about the job. Just like any other work colleagues in any other profession. Except our conversation went a bit like this:

'I don't know about you but my phone is dead at the moment.'

'Yeah, mine too. It's not school holidays, is it?'

'No. End of financial year, isn't it?'

'Oh yeah … Hey, did I tell you about Kevin, with the ginormous penis? Samantha, you've seen him too, he said you had.'

'Kevin? With the funny eye? God yes, don't tell me he's still with that awful girlfriend of his?'

'Yep! She made a pass at his son! What a cow!'

And so it went on. All afternoon, after two coffees and three servings of scones with whipped cream … and into the evening, with three bottles of Moët and only a few olives.

'And then … and then … we were having this threesome and you know what she's like, but she just gets up and sits on the loo for ages.'

'I wasn't! I was texting my boyfriend! I told him I was stuck on the freeway.'

'Bullshit, you were trying to kill time while I had to suck his dick on my own.'

'Well, he's your client and I'm sorry but his breath stinks ...'

'Well, how do you think his cock stank, you bitch! I'll get you back for that one!'

As the hours ticked by and groups of men eagerly hovered around, trying to catch our eyes, our voices got louder, our stories more outrageous.

'Oh my GOD, did you see that man just walk in?'

'The one with the nice arse?'

'Yes! Is he hot? Look at him, Sarah, what's his face like?'

'Oh no – not my type at all.'

'Sarah goes for obese taxi drivers.'

'Shut up! No, I don't!'

'You said you had the best sex of your life with that fat taxi driver client last week?'

'Yeah, but I hadn't had sex in ages and he had one of those bendy dicks that hit me in the right spot.'

We carried on with our bonding chatter until the barman laughed at us, shaking his head as we staggered to the lifts.

'Come on, I've got a suite, let's carry on up there,' Star slurred as she pressed the button for the fifteenth floor.

We stumbled into the lift, giggling and hiccupping as girls do, and fixed our faces in the mirror.

'We need to get into a bit of trouble,' slurred Ness. 'We've been far too well behaved.'

I nodded my head, high on Champagne and laughter. 'I know! It's only 9.30 p.m. I can't go to bed now, I've spent four hours today listening to the most boring engineer.'

Just then the lift stopped at level 1, where the conference rooms were. Business people were milling around on the landing, murmuring about how it was a good meeting, and which bar everyone was going to now.

A short, stout businessman with balding hair and a cheap suit marched into the lift energetically. Suddenly the small space stank of Lynx. His beady eyes lit up when he saw four tipsy women standing in front of him.

'G'day, ladies! I'm Bryce from Albury Wodonga.' He beamed enthusiastically, pointing to the white plastic name tag pinned on his canary polka-dot tie. 'Are youse all here for the accountancy convention?' He smiled while looking at each of us earnestly.

We looked at each other, our eyes all locking. *Yep.* We were on the same page; we knew what was coming. We were the same tribe. Poor Bryce. A case of wrong place at the wrong time, mate ...

'Do we look like fucking accountants, Bryce from Albury Wodonga?' Sarah winked before linking her arm through his. 'Come on, darling, you're coming with us.'

Before he knew what was happening, we each grabbed an arm or hand and lead him to Star's room.

'Jesus, girls, what's going on?' he blustered. 'You're not going to rob me, are you? I've got no money.'

'Shhhh, don't worry ... we're not going to hurt you,' whispered Ness in his ear. 'We're just going to have sex with you.'

'Jesus, girls! I'm a married man! I've been with my wife for thirty years! I've never even looked at another woman!' he feebly protested. 'Is there a camera here? Are youse girls winding me up? Or have I won the lotto?'

I couldn't help but laugh. Really laugh. Poor Bryce from Albury Wodonga: he had no idea what he was in for. Four office workers from the accountancy convention? Oh Bryce, my darling, we were drunk escorts fuelled by Champagne, a far more dangerous and wicked combination.

Being so perfect and interested in what men have to say, locked in a hotel room for hours, is a hard act to keep up sometimes. It's mentally draining being sensible and measured and 'on' all the time with clients – whichever job you have. We all need to let our hair down, don't we? And this, dear readers, is sometimes how escorts let their hair extensions down, especially when there are four of us.

Delivering a man for some fun was just what the hooker fairy ordered for us that night. And it just so happened that our plaything of choice was a chubby number cruncher from the country.

Mind you, and despite his protests, Bryce must have thought his gods were smiling on him that night as well. Grinning ear to ear, he threw his tatty rucksack on the carpet, kicked off his scuffed leather shoes and licked his lips. Star threw him onto the huge king-size bed and pulled his pants off.

'Look, girls! Bryce is wearing his lucky undies!' We all stood there giggling at his Homer Simpson silky boxers. 'Must be all the rage in Albury Wodonga!'

Even Bryce started laughing.

'The other ones were dirty!' he chirped, before he yanked them off himself. 'Jeez, girls, it's my lucky day ...' he said as Ness got on her knees and started devouring his tiny cock with her on plump lips.

'Don't worry, darling,' she breathed, coming up for air, her massive lips even more swollen. 'You're in very good hands. We are all *very* expensive escorts and you, my darling, are getting a freebie.' She popped her head down again and milked his now-hard cock.

'Me mates are not going to believe this one,' he moaned, his chubby hands around Ness's ponytail.

What happened next was a blur of naked women and one very stunned Bryce. I was sitting on Sarah's face, Bryce had his red face in Star's pussy while she had her fingers inside Sarah and Ness was trying to lick Bryce's balls ... and then in our drunken state we'd all swap over ...

It was all good fun until Star – who can't take her alcohol, because she's short, plus she wanted to go to sleep – suddenly got bored of Bryce.

'Psst, country boy,' she whispered. 'You're right, darling – there's a camera up there.' She pointed to some painting hanging on the wall.

Bryce suddenly pulled his penis out of Sarah and shot up onto his feet.

'You're bloody joking, aren't you? I knew it, I knew this was a wind-up. You don't know my full name, you don't know where I work. Youse girls have got nothing on me! Youse don't know anything!'

And before any of us could say 'Albury Wodonga', Bryce – with the condom still stuck on his dribbling penis – scrambled for his Simpson undies, yanked up his trousers, pulled his shirt on, and threw his jacket over his arm before running to the door.

'Youse girls are bloody mad,' he panted, looking back at us and shaking his head. 'Bloody mad.'

He slammed the door behind him, leaving us all sitting up naked in bed with a faint smell of Lynx lingering.

'Oh Star, that was really mean,' Sarah said, wiping her plump red lips. 'The poor bloke is going to worry about it now all night and think we're going to blackmail him.'

'As if! As if we would try to ruin his life,' I said, pulling myself up for a pee. 'We won't even remember his name tomorrow.' And as I walked to the bathroom I noticed something on the floor, just under the sofa where Bryce's jacket had lain. It was just a piece of paper – a scrap of rubbish, probably. It must have fallen out of his pocket in his haste to escape. It had writing on it. What did it say ...?

'Oh look, girls,' I cackled, bending down to pick it up. 'His business card!'

And there in black, white and red was a headshot of Bryce, red-faced and proud in his canary polka-dot tie, along with his full name, his phone number (and mobile) and his office address in, of course, Albury Wodonga.

CHAPTER 22

AMANDA

Break-ups and make-ups

So the cat was out of the bag. I couldn't exactly deny it – the evidence was there in black and white, and Big had it on his phone now. As for him remaining calm ... let's just say that bit was the calm before the storm. And that storm was a roaring category-5 cyclone.

Big wasn't calm about it at all, of course – he was absolutely ropable. And in the next few weeks he made his feelings towards me very, very clear.

You're a nasty gold digger ... How dare you use me ... Think of me did you when you were fucking Dan, did you?

So it went on. He even told me that he was going to release my clients' details on social media.

'I *told* you to stop taking his money,' Tab gently reminded me when I sobbed down the phone for the millionth time that week.

'I know, I can't believe I did it … I feel so terrible. He hates me. He'll never talk to me again.'

'Oh, he will,' Tab sighed. 'Unfortunately, he will.'

Funnily enough, after that I *did* stop working for a while. Not because of any reason except that I was too sad. How could I sit with a client when I'd done such an awful deed? How could I have taken Big's money? What was I thinking? Why couldn't I just have been honest with him?

The guilt weighed me down heavily. If I didn't feel bad as Samantha before, I sure as hell did now.

I hated my clients! I hated Samantha! She had so much to answer for! If she wasn't such a big force in my life, then I wouldn't be in this mess. If she wasn't so bloody defiant and headstrong, it wouldn't be so hard to leave her behind. And my clients! Why did they want to see me so much? Why couldn't they just find another girl and leave me ALONE!

Tab was right, of course: Big did talk to me again. He went from blocking me and ignoring me to telling me it was okay, that he still loved me and wanted me, and that we would work through it.

'I understand why you did it,' he said once. 'But how could you lie, Amanda? How could you lie to me?'

It was hard not to snap back, 'Well, pretty easily actually – I learnt from the best.' This was a man who was lying to everyone else in his life. He told his family he was at work dinners when he was with me; he told Scott, his best friend and colleague, that he was with his kids when he was with me. Phone calls from important people in his life went unanswered when he was with me.

As far as anyone else – like his sisters – was concerned, he went to London and Lake Como by himself. We even had a weekend away, snuggled together in the Mornington Peninsula – but according to his friends, he was at a work conference.

But me? He would insist he was my partner, my boyfriend, that I had to give up everything for him.

'I'll walk if you don't stop,' he said.

Why should I stop? For what? For being invisible? For being 'just some girl in the bar'?

I wasn't allowed to meet him in the city, close to his work, and I certainly wasn't allowed to go to any functions, work or family. Not even close to being on the guest list. When wedding invitations came in, they simply read 'To Big'. Not plus one or guest, because they just assumed he would be on his own, because he hadn't told them any different.

'They've put me on the singles table next to a hot blonde,' he joked when the millionth wedding invite turned up.

Really? You think that's funny, Big?

It was upsetting. It hurt.

I was the one who took the last flight out of Sydney to comfort him after his father died. *I* was the one who helped him through a tough time with a family member. *I* was the one who was supporting him emotionally, who sent him expensive handcrafted cards in the post telling him how much I loved him. *I* was the one filling up his fine china bowl with expensive organic bloody jelly beans and making sure his home was full of fresh flowers so it smelled nice.

Always knowing that as I was packing my suitcase, every single part of me had to be hidden away: my toothbrush, my spare pair of trainers. He would even check his pillow for my hairs.

'What's this?' he said once, exasperation in his voice, as he pulled one of my hair extensions from his bathroom bin. '*Amanda* ...'

If I 'insisted' on leaving anything at his house, he was meticulous at hiding it. Sometimes, when I was feeling brave, I'd secrete a lipstick in his bathroom cabinet, behind the big bottle of Aveda shampoo. Or I'd shove my plane ticket, with my name boldly emblazoned on it, in the side-door pocket of his car underneath all the packets of chewing gum. Once I even stuffed my G-string in the pocket of his suit. He'd *have* to tell Scott about me then!

But with his eagle eye he would always find whatever it was, take it and hide it, or throw it away. 'You're crazy, Amanda,' he'd say, 'but that's why I love you.'

Actually, it wasn't me being crazy.

It was me being tragically desperate.

My fantasy of being part of his life had been chipped away slowly, along with my confidence. Over time, I realised I was always going to be a secret. Sure, I could put him down as my NOK, but no one else in his life could know and god forbid if he was ever needed as my NOK – he'd probably lie about where he was. 'Um ... just at the gym,' he'd fib to his friends while helping paramedics pick my crumpled body off the side of the road.

Quite frankly, that didn't do wonders for my self-esteem, that idea – again – of *not being good enough.*

So how could I lie to him? Actually, yeah, pretty easily.

How can I trust you now, Amanda? said one of his many text messages a few weeks later.

Interesting question.

He was the one who made up aliases to try to trick me out – and then swore on so-and-so's life that it wasn't him. He even dropped it into conversations that other escorts – escorts he had seen previously – had contacted him and wanted to see him.

'I just ignored her,' he said, to reassure me. 'But look!' And he would show me emails from girls: *Hi handsome, in town again, fancy a hook-up?*

A few times he emailed an escort to book an appointment, then cancelled at the last minute – 'To show you how it feels,' he said. And if I got upset, I would be labelled a hypocrite or mad or jealous. Or even worse: 'I just made it up to play with you.'

Of course, that would send me into a quietly terrified, insecure mess. Big had a huge sex drive, and as I lived in Sydney, I couldn't always be there. So in the back of my head, I worried (or did I know, really?) that he was fucking other women too.

So how could he trust *me*?

He was the one who had no problem lying to every single person in his life about me.

How could he trust me?

'How can I trust *you*, Big?'

'For god's sake, Amanda, I told you that would take time – I told you in time – time would heal ...'

'I got sick of waiting, Big, I'm sorry.'

And it went round and round in one big circle for weeks. Awful fighting, great sex, awful fighting, great sex.

'I still love you, godammit, Amanda,' Big groaned as he slid on top of me. 'I hate the fact I still love you.'

And he would force his hardness into me, plunge deeper and deeper, knowing the sheer size of his swollen cock would open me up and bruise me, punishing me for my crime.

'Big, you're hurting me,' I moaned quietly in his ear, trying to push him off.

'Too bad,' came his snarly reply. *Take it. Suck it up, princess.*

My punishment was going to last for months.

CHAPTER 23

SAMANTHA

When the wife calls

It was bound to happen, wasn't it. Six years as an escort, and not once had I been on the receiving end of a phone call from a client's wife.

Until one recent Tuesday afternoon.

I had just come back from my delicious week's retreat in Queensland, relaxed, healthy – and my nails looking *far* too natural for an escort's. They needed tips, length and a splash of colour – something sexy ... a deep, dark red this time.

Just as my nail technician, Kim, was tutting at my talons, a text message came through from my business partner, Vanessa.

I've just had a lady called Stephanie on the phone. She said you have had sex with her husband and wants to speak to you. I think her husband's name is Gerry. I said I would pass on the message and she said she would greatly appreciate if you called her back. I'll send the number.

Oh shit: so my time had come. If there was one way to have my anxiety levels shoot up after a retreat, it was this.

And as Kim pulled on her mask to avoid breathing in the acrylic fumes, I sat there with one hand clutching my phone as the other was being filed, wondering what the hell was I going to say to this Stephanie. I'd play it by ear, gauge how angry she was ... I could call her when I got home, but these nails would take an hour ... and I was too curious.

'Hello, Stephanie? This is Samantha. You rang ...'

'Oh Samantha, thanks for calling back. I really appreciate it.' I heard the relief in her voice straightaway. She was well spoken, with a mild Australian accent. If you could picture a woman by her voice, she sounded blonde and petite.

'So my husband saw you two years ago. I've seen the emails.'

Phew. No raised voices so far.

'Okay ...' I said slowly.

'He told you he was an engineer but really he's a doctor,' Stephanie said. 'He's fair haired and short. He would have been wearing a navy suit.'

'Sorry, he isn't ringing any bells.'

Oh god, who was he? She clearly expected me to remember.

'He saw you for an hour? Paid cash?'

'Yes, but it was a long time ago. You say two years ago? I'm sorry, Stephanie, I don't know whether that makes you happy or whether I am insulting you, but I have actually no idea who your husband is.'

Shit, should I have said that?

She laughed.

'Yes, that's him! Pretty unmemorable!'

We laughed together. Then I stopped: this wasn't supposed to be funny.

'He told me he booked you for the intimacy, not the sex,' she said. 'He told me he booked you for the cuddling.'

'Okay.'

'You don't remember?'

No, I really don't!

For a split second, I thought maybe I should lie to make her feel better. Say, yes, I do remember her short and fair-haired husband in his navy suit; yes, she married someone *extremely* memorable ...

But I didn't. I had no idea who she was talking about. Whether she would be insulted by that I didn't know, but it was the truth.

'Okay, doesn't matter,' Stephanie said, her voice flat. 'I understand – you've probably seen hundreds of men.'

Was that a dig?

'Well, I wouldn't say hundreds ...'

'But lots of men since him.'

'Yes.'

'You know, Samantha, it broke my heart when I found out.'

Ouch. There it was: the stab of guilt. I had something to do with a woman's pain. *I hate this feeling.*

'You weren't the only one, he'd been seeing others too.'

'Right.'

Why did that irk me that I wasn't the only one?

'We were trying for a baby at the time. Trying for a baby! Can you believe that?'

'Wow. What a bastard. I am so sorry to hear this, Stephanie.'

I did feel sorry for her but when it came to men, nothing surprised me. I've had clients who saw me two days before their wedding; who slept in my bed as their wife was breastfeeding their newborn twins. One whose wife had just been diagnosed with cancer; one whose wife was *dying*.

I once had a client who was on holiday in Sydney with his wife – he asked me to come to the hotel while she was at Westfield.

I've had men tell outright lies to their families in front of me. A lot of men tell lies to their loved ones about what they do during the day. 'So I had the monthly performance review, then had Chinese for lunch, then spent two hours in a hotel with an escort, then went back to work and made it home just in time for dinner! How was *your* day, darling?' As a wife, have you ever heard your husband say that? Didn't think so.

To recap: nothing these men did was a shock to me anymore.

'I just couldn't understand where all this money was going,' Stephanie continued. 'I mean, I don't spend a thing! We have a nice life, but I'm not one of these women who spends all their husband's money ... Well, I am now. Once I found out he was spending $1000 an hour on you, I made sure he spends triple that on me – don't you think that's right?'

'Absolutely! Make sure you absolutely spend his money! Buy those shoes, demand more diamonds! It's the least he can do.'

'I know! He was always texting to say he was running late. So I started to suspect.'

Aha: women's intuition. A dangerous thing, and never wrong.

Is Big still fucking escorts?

'So I called the bank to get his credit card statements.'

'They're stupid, aren't they, men?'

'Yes, they are. He'd been doing it for years, Samantha. Years! Well, he broke down when I confronted him. He was very, very upset and begged me not to leave him.'

'And you haven't, obviously?'

'No, but I'm finding it hard.' She went quiet.

'Of course you are. I can't imagine how hard it would be.' I felt guilty: I was the 'other woman'. She had probably told her girlfriends about these 'other women' who had fucked her husband – and I was one of them.

'He was so upset that I had to tell his family. He needed someone as support. I was worried about what he was going to do.'

'Oh god, what a mess.'

'It's been very stressful. I never thought it would happen to us. We had a good marriage!'

I thought about what to say next. She was being very honest with me and I felt she deserved the same in return.

'Some men do it because they just need variety,' I said, 'not because the marriage is broken.'

She was quiet for a few seconds. 'Oh really?'

'Yes. Try not to blame yourself.'

'I don't, but it's not easy. I have a question, Samantha, if you don't mind me asking?'

'Not at all, please ask me anything you like, Stephanie. I would like to help.'

'Thank you.' She paused. 'I just want to know. How can you, as an escort, cuddle a man like my husband without feeling anything for him?'

That was it? That was all she wanted to know? What about the sex? The kissing? The sweet nothings he could have whispered? She just wanted to know about the cuddling? That broke my heart, her simple question. It was not the sex that hurt the most but the intimacy. I understood that. For her husband to wrap his arms around another woman and breathe in her perfume, her smell – yes, I could see how that hurt. I looked at Kim furrowing her brow at my nails and bit my lip. And again, more guilt.

'The cuddling? Oh, um ...'

Well, gosh – that was one question I hadn't been asked before. And as my nails were being buffed and polished, I sat back and thought about my answer carefully. One wrong word could change her day. Could change her *marriage*.

'You see, Stephanie –'

'Call me Steph.'

'You see, Steph, I mean, I like my clients – all of them. I haven't had one I didn't like, so it's not like I don't like them …'

Silence.

That sounded terrible. She was probably anxiously sitting at her kitchen table in her nice home, with a cup of tea or a glass of wine, waiting for my pearls of wisdom, for my wise sex-worker words. And what the hell was I trying to say? Even I didn't know. But I had to say something.

'Look, it's easy, okay?' I pressed on. 'I can cuddle them because it is my job. I get paid a lot of money to do it. All men who come to see me have needs – usually non-sexual – whether it's cuddling or stroking or telling me about their lonely marriages. So while the cuddling sometimes is harder than the sex, it's just my job. I don't need to have feelings for them, or for your husband. Just like the male doctor doesn't have feelings for the patient he does a Pap smear on. It's a job – nothing less, nothing more.'

Why can't Big understand that? It would make my life easier if he could.

'So you can cuddle a client without feeling something?' She sounded disbelieving.

'Yes! I mean, obviously I think he's a nice bloke who may be going through some kind of tough time. Human to human, I feel compassion for my clients. But not feelings per se.'

'He told me he did it because of the cuddling,' she said. 'I suppose, looking back, we were fighting a lot at the time. I wanted a baby and was pretty focused on that. I admit I wasn't the easiest person to live with.'

'It's not your fault, Steph. Men can be selfish. Don't ever blame yourself.'

'They are, aren't they! That's one thing I've learned, Samantha: my husband is bloody selfish. They all are. How do you have faith in men?'

Good question. I don't trust Big.

'It's not easy. But not all men do it. They *all* think about it, I'm sure about that, but I don't think they *all* mess around.'

'Really?'

'Yes. But, remember, I only see the ones who do.'

'True! So what do you actually think when you are cuddling them?'

I'm thinking about Big. But I can't tell her that.

'I'm thinking about what to have for dinner,' I fibbed, 'whether I should take the dogs for a walk when I get home or go to F45 instead, I'm thinking how tight this lingerie is and I can't wait to put my tracksuit on: I'm thinking how long I'll have to cuddle him for before I pop him in the shower. Sometimes I don't really think of anything. I am certainly not thinking about how much I like your husband and how I want to prise him away from you.'

Seconds ticked by.

'Thank you,' she said at last.

'And when your husband or any other client leaves, I don't think about him,' I said. 'I don't remember half of them.'

'Oooh, I am not sure he would like that!' she said.

We laughed.

'There was no crazy sex with my husband?'

'Steph, I could count on one hand the times I've had crazy sex with a client and your husband wasn't one of them! It's rarely about the sex. The sex is the cherry on top and usually it's vanilla. It's about the intimacy.'

'There's no handcuffs and whips?'

I snorted, giggling. Kim snarled at me. I'd smudged my nail polish and now there was a stripe of deep red sticky polish on my finger. 'Sorry,' I mouthed.

'No, sadly,' I said to Stephanie. 'I don't get those clients. The sex is just normal run-of-the-mill sex. Clients may think they're booking an escort for sex, but quite often the time together turns into a bit of a therapy session.'

Stephanie sighed.

'I suppose I didn't want to hear about his problems,' she said. 'I was going through a tough time with this baby thing ...'

'Of course, I understand. I am paid to listen, remember.'

'He says he's stopped, that he will never be with an escort again, that he is so sorry he's hurt me. All the money he's saved on hookers ... sorry, escorts ... he's bought himself a sports car! But I don't trust him, Samantha. I track his phone and –'

'Whoa – hang on, you track his phone?'

'Yes, and I was thinking of getting a private investigator.'

Yes, I thought of that too at one stage.

'Stop. Steph, I'm going to be honest with you: you absolutely cannot live like that. That will send you insane. That is no way for any woman to live.'

So why didn't I listen to my own advice?

'I know,' she said, her voice wavering.

'You have two choices. You either decide to trust him and move on – he has to earn your trust again, of course. Or you leave. But you cannot spend the rest of your life worrying.'

'But I'm forty-two – I haven't worked for years. I'd have to start again.' She sniffled. 'Tell me, Samantha, what would you do if you were me?'

Was that desperation in her voice? I felt such empathy for this woman. We've all been there, haven't we? We've all felt such utter helpless desperation that we plead with strangers for advice, hoping they'll somehow know the answer, that they will solve our problems for us.

I'll tell you if you tell me, Steph. What do you think I should do with Mr Big? Can you help me? Please? Because I have no bloody idea about my own relationship, let alone solving yours.

Instead I said, 'What would *I* do? Gosh, I don't know. I avoid relationships, that's what I do!'

'Don't blame you,' she murmured in agreement. 'Do you think he will stop?'

No. No. No. Absolutely not. Once a punter, always a punter. But I had to word it a bit more delicately than that.

'Steph, woman to woman, do I think he will stop? The answer is no. I think he will stop for a few months, maybe a few years. But the temptation is too great. It's the thrill he may miss – the excitement of booking a girl, walking to the hotel, the anticipation ... I feel bad saying this to you, but in my experience the ones that get caught always go back.'

So does that mean Big will never stop? I wanted to ask her: do you think Big has stopped? Should I put a tracking device on him?

'So you think I should leave?'

I don't know; do you think I should?

'Steph, I think you actually know your answer, deep down.'

Do I? Do I know my answer deep down? I love Big ... but is love enough?

'You're probably right,' Steph said. 'You know, my psychologist said that some women in my position end up working as escorts!'

We both laughed, and her voice sounded lighter.

'Well, give me a call if you decide to do that,' I said. 'That would show your husband, wouldn't it? Let him wonder where *you* are for a change!'

'I'd need to lose weight,' she said softly.

'Don't be silly. I am sure you're beautiful as you are.'

She sighed. 'Samantha, thank you. Our conversation has really helped me.'

'I hope so, Steph. If you have any more questions, anything you forgot to ask, just call me. I'll help you in any way I can. It's the least I can do.'

'Thank you.'

Thank you.

I smiled at Kim as I hung up but she only scowled back.

———

So, that was it: a real, raw conversation between the escort and the wife. I'm not going to say 'poor Steph' because she didn't want to be a victim. She was a woman who was searching for answers.

Should she stay in her marriage or leave? No one could answer that apart from Steph. But what I can tell you is that the answer is always complex. I felt guilty that I'd had a part to play in her pain. But I had meant what I said: it really is just a job.

I'm not going to stop working because of the hurt it could cause to a partner. I don't choose the men – they choose me. Someone else's marriage is none of my business. And who are we to judge her husband? He was clearly going through his own issues. It was a fucked-up situation, but it is happening to couples all around Australia and the world. Not one single person was to blame: not me, not her husband and certainly not Steph.

Part of me wished I could have sat with them in a room and helped them deal with their issues. In fact, sometimes when I'm with a client and I hear the things he says about his wife and their marriage, I wish I could find a way to let her hear it. Shagging escorts isn't a way to solve your problems; neither is asking them for advice.

If I was so bloody good at relationships, then I wouldn't be in this mess with Big. Would I?

CHAPTER 24

AMANDA

Hi ho, hi ho, it's off to work we go

Once the dust had settled and the punishing sex eased off, Big and I did what most couples do: put one massive bandaid on our issues and started again.

While I felt terrible about hurting him, it was hard not to feel relieved that it was all out in the open. Big cut off the money, obviously, and I could go back to work.

I offered him the chance to have an open relationship, but he said no.

'I don't want anyone else, Amanda,' he explained. 'I was happy about that because I didn't want to date either. Work was work. I did it for money and freedom, not desire. Dating was a different ball game.

And with our renewed relationship came a fresh new rule – a rule of honesty.

'It's the lies I can't bear, Amanda,' Big said. 'Just don't lie to me.'

Okay, that was fair enough. And of course, there should be no lying to me either.

Work picked up again, and I was back to seeing my old regulars like Mark and J and Mr Nice, this time, without the constant checking of my phone and gnawing of my nails.

The fact that, really, nothing had changed and I was still no closer to meeting Big's family still lurked in the pit of my stomach – but how could I blame him now? He was right: I had done a terrible thing and taken myself back to square one. I had to earn my place in his life all over again.

'Darling, I've got dinner with Mr Nice, I'm just letting you know,' I'd tell Big before a job.

'No problem.'

'Love you.'

'Love you too.'

He seemed to be okay with it. And I hated lying: it was confusing, it was difficult and it made me feel like shit. I didn't want to put myself through that again. Thank god Big could be sensible about all this now. Thank god he finally understood that me working was about me having my own independence. Thank god he finally understood that I didn't love my clients, nor did they have my heart. He was the one I loved, he was the one who had my heart, he was the one I wanted to be with ...

Except his understanding didn't last very long. We would have a fight, usually about me posting something on my social media pages that inflamed him (a necessary evil in my line of work) or about a dinner date with a regular client, and his jealousy would erupt and explode in abusive, pointed text messages.

Fuck another client last night then? How was it? How can you do this to me?

Or:

No man will ever want you ... you're nothing but a tragic hooker with nothing else in her life.

Or:

Why should you be the only one fucking? I've got choices too. You lied to me, after all ...

Or:

You don't deserve to be a part of my life!

And when you are constantly bombarded by messages like that, it is extremely hard not to feel broken.

So, much to the despair of Vanessa and Tab and everyone else who cared for me, I slid away into my shell again. I lost my sparkle and joy, and upped my counselling sessions with Doris to twice a week.

'Get rid of him, Amanda!' Tab would plead with me. 'This is always going to be your relationship! He is never going to change, you're never going to change – when will you see that?'

She banned him from her house, and, while she was sick to death of seeing me sad, she was always the first person I'd call. Once I turned up at her house after a particularly bad fight with Big, with happy balloons and bright pink gifts for her daughter's birthday party.

'Happy birthday!' I smiled weakly, holding up the balloons to cover my anguished face, before bursting into tears in front of all the guests. Tab promptly put me in her bed, made me tea and gave me a Valium, her silent anger towards Big and her frustration at the situation seeping from her pores. But she was always there for me. Always.

If I tried to end it, if I tried to leave, Big would always come back with a million more messages, flowers, gifts, promises that he loved me and that things would change soon. *I can't live without you. I need you.*

And things would smooth over again.

Until that night. That night after the cinema, where we kissed on the pavement as people jostled by. That night where he googled the plates and Wendy West popped up on his search engine.

Until that night where I found out he had been fucking other escorts anyway: Wendy West, Sarah Smith and god knows who else. Right under my very nose. The same weeks I'd been with him in Melbourne. Until that night where I found out that since I'd met him, he had never stopped sleeping with escorts. *He had never stopped.*

On that night my heart, which was wobbly at the best of times, well and truly broke in two.

CHAPTER 25

SAMANTHA

My friends

When I first came out publicly, with all guns blazing, on Channel Seven's *Sunday Night* show, it was a shock to quite a few people. Not my family – I'd warned them; not my girlfriends, not anyone close to me. Even Reuven, my barista, knew. But, sure, ex-work colleagues, my editors and fellow reporters were frothing at the mouth over this juicy exclusive. Amanda Goff – a hooker! Who would have thought it! (It turned out no one was really that shocked ...)

But the group of people who were probably more shocked than anyone was my very own tribe: the sex workers.

Who is this Samantha X?

She claims to have been an escort for years but we haven't heard of her!

Does she even exist?

I bet she made the whole thing up to get publicity for her book!

And I don't blame them one iota for thinking that.

Samantha X had never been on any social media – there was no Twitter, not even an Instagram page. My profile had never been seen on any of the popular websites where all escorts advertised. It wasn't a huge industry and, the thinking went, someone *surely* would have heard of me. But, nope, they were utterly perplexed as to who this Samantha was.

Even clients on punter websites discussed how they didn't believe Samantha X ever really existed, that she wasn't a real person, and it was all a clever publicity stunt.

I had journalists calling me up asking me if I had lied about the whole thing. I did joke to one female reporter that it was a hell of a tough thing to put myself through for the fun of it. Didn't they know I was a terrible liar?

They were right, though: Samantha X *hadn't* existed until that evening I came out on TV.

And do you want to know why?

Because I used to work under a different name. I used to be called Vanessa and I never showed my face in my photos.

I had been Vanessa for years, even at the Bordello, where I was eventually firmly shown the door.

I decided to rename and repackage myself with the publication of my book, and so Samantha X was born. The X was my 'I'll fill in this blank bit later' to my publishers; I'd planned to come up with a cool surname. But I sort of forgot about it, and the X stayed.

So when I came out guns blazing with a 'fuck-you' attitude about being an escort and proud of it, I made one major mistake. One mistake that I didn't realise I'd made until recently: I didn't try to make an effort to get to know my peers. I didn't reach out to them to introduce myself, to make a few fellow escort friends, a few allies. And if I am really truthful about it, that was because I didn't think their opinion of me mattered that much. As I was banging on about how society needed to stop judging sex workers, I was the one guilty of being judgmental.

I didn't need any friends in the industry! How could I trust any of them? Weren't they all out to steal my clients? Didn't they all bitch about me when I came out? *Pah!* I didn't need their help, their support! They weren't the ones paying my bills. It was men I had to attract – future clients I wanted to snare. It was the public I had to woo, not women in the sex industry – not my competition. I didn't need them! I didn't need any of them!

As far as I was concerned, other escorts were a bunch of bitchy bullies who didn't say nice things about anybody.

How wrong was I.

How arrogant was I.

How misguided was I.

How lonely it felt to be in this challenging industry with no support from women living it too.

Sure, there is the small minority of grumbling, bitter women who will always be grumbling and bitter about other women. But there are a hell of a lot more who aren't like that.

I'm going to admit to something that I should have realised two years ago: that I needed their support. That the women I have had the honour of meeting in this industry have been the kindest, most genuine, compassionate and intelligent women I've met in any industry. That I should have reached out. That they weren't out to 'get me' nor wanted to see me fail. That the majority are simply smart businesswomen who cheer other women on, who offer support when we need it, who do everything in their power to make our industry a safe one, who want all women to feel empowered and be successful. I will try to mention all the women I love, cherish and respect – if I've left your name out, I apologise.

Kimber Slone, an extremely smart, sexy and savvy escort in Brisbane, showed me loyalty and kindness when I was having tough times with Big. She had no reason to – she didn't know me from a bar of soap. She had never met me. But one day, after she read some post I put up on Twitter about something silly, she called me and said hello: 'Loved your post! Fancy a coffee one day?' And we have been good friends ever since. She is a whiz in business, super smart, and if I ever need financial advice, she is one of the first I call. We bumped into each other quite accidentally at some five-star resort, me with my kids, her with a client.

'Samantha?' she whispered at the breakfast buffet.

'Kimber?' I whispered back. And we bonded even more.

The hysterically funny and beautiful Amanda Valentina made me laugh over our espresso coconut milk smoothies, often taking time out of her stressful touring/eating cuisine schedule to check in to see how I was coping after the Big break-up. Again, I count her as someone I would call if upset. Without going into details, she has shown me more integrity than any female work colleague I had in the media.

Escorts know. They get it. They understand. We've all had our hearts broken; most of us have dated clients. We understand. We are the *only* ones who can understand us. We are complex – we know we are complex – but to each other we are easy to understand.

Along with Sienna James, who is wildly intelligent for her young age, and Holly Hazel, who has a kind heart and makes me laugh, I enjoyed a sensible brunch in Perth before getting pissed. That turned into Holly streaking in the middle of a rugby game and me accosting male joggers in the dark, while Sienna, the youngest of our trio, tried to control the situation. Somehow we all ended up naked in my bath ... but that will be in book number three.

Evelyn May and Lola Grace, both tattooed models (and I mean *really* tattooed!) were not as tough as they looked but instead were softly spoken, smart and gentle women who were gorgeous on the inside as well as the out.

Madison Missina, Jessica Bardot and Brooke Beauford have shown me kindness and support; Dominique Diaz reached out when the bullying hit an all-time peak and told a few girls to back off. Then Anna Ferraro stuck up for me online when I was under fire from the trolls, and she hadn't even met me.

Another escort, Eden Love – again who I had never met – texted to say she just laughed and ignored it when the trolls attacked me. *I know you're a big girl and thick skin doesn't come easy, so good for you. Sending whore love your way!* she wrote. We had lunch together just before she gave birth.

Lady Jayme, who I've never met, sends me messages of kindness and support, from boob-job chat to advice on dodgy clients. The beautiful Adela Blackwood makes me laugh; Angelina Rose is a true beauty; Rene Jolie took me for a spin in her Porsche. I've connected with escorts all over the world, too: Sophia West from the states, porn stars from LA ...

Kyla Winter is one of my closest friends. We take it in turns to cry over men together (boyfriends, not clients – the clients never make us cry), and we try to make each other laugh in threesomes. Actually, we can't even look at each other when we are working together as we always dissolve into fits of giggles.

Estelle Lucas is a young and ferociously smart escort. Natalie Jade and I call each other up whingeing about men. Aubrey Black is a beautiful, smart woman I look up to. And it's not just women: male escorts Ryan James and Jake Ryan, I salute you for understanding the needs of women. Websites like Scarlet Blue and Private Girls provide an intelligent and well-respected way of connecting clients to workers.

The list could go on and on. If I am feeling down, or sad or anxious, or I simply don't know how to handle a situation, there are plenty of women I would call now, who I trust and respect, and I am always happy to help when I can too. I feel blessed to be part of such a strong sisterhood, and I am glad I realised that by ignoring my peers or not really giving a shit as to what *they* thought, I was only isolating one person – and that was *me*.

To the dear, dear women in the sex industry, I want to say thank you for reaching out, thank you for your friendship and thank you for the nights we all end up naked together high on Moët and being together. We don't have an easy job, we know it's not all Champagne, roses and sweet nothings. It's draining and challenging, and most of us live in fear of being outed and excluded by friends and family. But we are the same tribe, we face the same issues and we would drop anything to help one of our own. I know my circle would.

And, more importantly, we are all equal. No one is better than anyone else. We are all unique and we are not in competition. We cater to every man's taste. I'm certainly not everyone's cup of tea – I can't compete with a taut, toned 20-year-old, but I don't want to either. Men like variety. Isn't that the spice of life? You learn not to take it personally.

I cherish my friendships with these women and my life has only been richer with them in it. If I ever left the sex industry, I don't think I could ever leave these women behind. We share a bond that no one will ever understand. And I didn't really understand it. Until now.

CHAPTER 26

SAMANTHA

Girls' night out

Just when you think nothing else in this job could possibly surprise me, it did. Just when I thought I had crossed off the funniest stories and client goings-on on my Qantas sick bag (I always scribble notes when I am flying), another unbelievable event occurred in Samantha's life.

I say unbelievable because, quite frankly, you will probably not believe it happened. But it did, at a rooftop hotel bar in Melbourne. Of course it was in my beloved Melbourne. City of great times and terrible hangovers.

It was a Wednesday evening. Mark, my kinky client, had booked me and another escort, Evelyn, for a few hours. I can name her because she said I could, and if you google her, you'll see she is very pretty, smart and tattooed – and I count her as a good friend.

Nothing particularly exciting was happening at the rooftop bar; just a few cocktails and mingling. Except Evelyn and I weren't mingling – Mark was.

Evelyn and I were at the bar when we turned round to see Mark sitting at a table, laughing and clinking glasses with two women dressed in conservative business suits (Cue, not Chanel). Normal-looking curvy women with nice hair and lipstick, aged in their late thirties, both wearing wedding rings and sensible shoes.

'What the fuck?' I said, putting my glass down. 'Mark's picking up!'

Evelyn spun around and almost spat her drink out. 'We're not good enough, are we?' she said with a grin.

We sat and watched, bemused, as he touched their shoulders, poured them wine from the bottle and listened intently when they spoke.

'Bloody hell, Evie, we've been demoted!' I giggled, nudging her elbow. 'Either that or he wants a gang bang.'

Just then Mark turned around and winked at me, making a subtle thumbs-up sign under the table so we could see.

Evie and I locked eyes.

'Oh, Jesus Christ,' I murmured. 'Of course he does. I

knew it was too good to be true. Mark wants a bloody gang bang.' Why is it never simple with that man?

Evie rolled her eyes. 'With those women? Is he serious? They're married for a start – as if ...'

'Girls,' Mark excitedly interrupted us, sidling up to us at the bar. 'You need to work your magic! Samantha, offer them $1000 each to spend a few hours with us upstairs. Explain who you are and what you do.'

'Mark, but ...' I protested feebly. Seriously? These two office workers were probably having a quick drink before meeting their husbands then probably have something sensible for dinner like protein and salad. As if they would want a bloody gang bang with two escorts and some strange bloke. This wasn't Disneyland, Mark ...

'Come on! It will be fun! It's an adventure!' His eyes were dancing as he tapped me on the bum.

There was no point arguing with Mark. For a start, he was a lawyer. Second, he was my best regular. Third, I had Evelyn as back-up.

'Okay,' I sighed reluctantly. 'Come on, Evie, you're coming with me.'

Here goes ... what? A drink in my face?

'Ladies,' I said brightly, 'good evening, my name is Samantha, and this is my girlfriend Evelyn.' I smiled boldly. 'May we join you?'

They both looked up, frowning. 'Er … sure?' the blonde said. 'I'm Eloise and this is my friend Catherine.'

We chatted for a while. They worked in consulting in an office block up the road; both were married, one had a baby.

'Oh, she's beautiful!' I smiled as I was shown photos of her husband and child.

Out of the corner of my eye I could feel Mark's gaze burning into me; his cock was probably twitching with excitement.

I cleared my throat. 'Look, girls, I'm going to cut to the chase: Evelyn and I are escorts.'

They both looked at each other – then smiled.

'Oh wow!' Eloise said. 'Escorts, really?'

'And you have been talking to my dear client Mark,' I went on. 'And if I may, Catherine …' I leaned into her ear and whispered, 'Mark wants to offer you and your girlfriend $1000 cash each to join us all upstairs for Champagne … absolutely no pressure to have sex …'

'Oh,' they both said.

'Really?' said Catherine.

'He's your client?' said Eloise.

'Wow …'

'A thousand dollars cash? For the whole night?'

'Eloise, there's that LV wallet you saw in David Jones ...'

'Oh yeah! I really want it ... but shit – what would my husband say?'

'But I'm fat.'

'I haven't waxed and I'm really hairy.'

'I don't feel sexy, my husband never wants sex.'

'I'm wearing these disgusting fat knickers.'

'I've got a scar where I had my caesarean.'

'My tights have holes in them.'

Then they both looked at each other, before looking at me and clinking their Champagne glasses.

'Fuck it. Let's do it.'

Evelyn and I looked at each other. Had we heard right?

'Yeah, go on then – why not!' Eloise grinned, picking up her bag.

Unbloodybelieveable.

So they had agreed. These two normal women having a quiet drink after work had agreed to come up to a hotel room with a client and two escorts for cash.

I think Evelyn and I were more shocked than Mark was. I gave Mark the nod (why couldn't things ever be simple with him?), and we piled in the elevator to the sixth floor, where Mark had his suite.

'Now remember, girls, anytime you feel uncomfortable and want to leave, you leave,' I said carefully. The last thing

I needed was a court case on my hands about how I had coerced two innocent women upstairs.

I needn't have worried.

As soon as we opened the door to Mark's hotel room, Catherine and Eloise flung off their sensible business suits, kicked off their sensible shoes and jumped on the bed. They were right: they needed a wax, their tights did have holes in them, and their lingerie wasn't matching. But that did not slow them down one iota.

'Throw the cash all over my naked body!' Catherine yelled, lying on her back with her legs open as Mark flicked green notes all over her flesh. 'I want to feel like a hooker tonight!'

Eloise, the more liberated of the two, took all her clothes off and started pashing Catherine. Mark kicked off his shoes and joined in. Evelyn and I tried to make an effort but we kept getting shoved and bumped off the bed, so we put on the dressing gowns, poured a drink and watched, half in shock but mostly highly amused that these two married women needed zero encouragement to 'act like hookers tonight'.

The next few hours were a bit of a blur of endless Champagne flowing, lingerie flying everywhere, bodies writhing on crisp white sheets.

That was them, by the way, not Evelyn and me. We just sat on the sofa feeling ridiculously redundant and, quite frankly, more like amused spectators of the drunken orgy.

Midnight passed and one of the women's phones beeped.

'My husband wants to know where I am,' Eloise said, checking her phone as she came up from sucking Mark's cock to get air.

In a hotel room with two hookers, she texted back.

No, really where are you? was his response.

She threw the phone back on the bed before bobbing her head in between Mark's legs again, as Catherine lay there playing with herself.

One hour, two hours, three hours later ...

If you don't come home now, I won't respect you anymore, said another message.

That one was ignored.

And so it went on. Rolling around on the bed with Mark was interrupted by filling up their Champagne glasses and quizzing Evelyn and me about our jobs.

'So tell us about your funny experiences!'

'We can't believe you get paid to do this!'

'I told my husband I wanted to be a stripper once!'

'Escorting is so much fun!'

'I've never felt so sexy in my life!'

'My husband is going to kill me.'

'You're not going to tell him, are you?'

I couldn't help but laugh. I am so used to seeing men cheat, men lie, men do sneaky, naughty things, that it was so refreshing and so wickedly funny that these women needed little encouragement to break a few rules. It was as if they felt free, empowered, sexy. It was as if they had left their insecurities at the door and felt comfortable enough to be sexually free in front of complete strangers.

Eloise was the loudest of the two. She obviously had a penchant for pain as she kept slapping Mark and pulling his hair, which he loved. Catherine was more shy, more conservative. She kept her panties on, but the bra came off, and her laddered tights ended up as a crumpled heap on the floor.

I kept checking in with them, to make sure they were okay, and kept reminding them that they could leave at any time ...

'Samantha, if you please, Catherine and I need a word with you in the bathroom,' Eloise said, grabbing my hand.

Oh shit, here we go ...

'You want to leave? Of course!' I said. 'I hope Mark isn't making you feel uncomfortable..'

She looked at me solemnly as Catherine sat on the loo, shaking her head.

'Samantha, Catherine and I are in trouble,' she said seriously.

'You are?' I stammered. 'Your husbands know where you are? Has Mark done something?'

'No. Our problem is that we are enjoying this,' she said. 'Enjoying it a little too much. I am worried I am going to want to do this again ...'

CHAPTER 27

AMANDA

It's complicated

God, you must be tearing your hair out by now. 'Leave Big, Amanda! He's an arsehole!' – is that what you're thinking? Either that or you are completely bored by the drama. I wouldn't blame you, because I was too and so was everyone else in my life. I had finally had enough.

So you'll be pleased to know I *did* end it that night I found out about Wendy West. I threw myself into Samantha, the woman who I knew would rescue me, and you know what? She did.

I began to remember how much I enjoyed my job without Big breathing down my neck, without rushing to the loo to answer his texts. I remembered how exciting it was going on tour and meeting new clients – nothing beats that feeling of gliding through a hotel lobby wondering who is going to be behind the door.

I started to pay more attention to my appearance again.

'My ex-boyfriend is an arsehole, make me look happy again,' I said to my cosmetic surgeon, who nodded and smiled as if he'd heard this many, many times from women sitting in his reclining chair, with pain they wanted to erase from their faces.

Two grand later, fine Botox needles had stung my face, each one a reminder of the pain I was masking. Whatever it would take, I would do it.

I spent a fortune on lingerie; I announced new tour dates. I tried new cities, excitedly booked new hotels. Vanessa was delighted – she could start throwing herself into our business again, to build the Samantha X brand without me constantly changing my mind or deleting social media posts. And I felt something I hadn't felt in a long time – empowerment!

I was coming back to life. Like an ice cube thawing in the sun, the sadness was leaving me. Apart from a few messages here and there, after he knew he wasn't going to get anywhere – that I was over it and over him – He disappeared. My phone was finally silent; the emails also stopped. And it was time to concentrate on Samantha.

Of course, I had days where I stayed in bed crying, or sometimes tortured myself by painstakingly studying the profiles of the other escorts he had fucked. Was she prettier than me? Was she better in bed? Was she in love with him too? Or, worse: was he in love with her? What if *she'd* met his friends? What if *she'd* met his family?

But that was part of the process. That was the many stages of grief. The relationship was over and I was healing.

Weeks, months passed. But without any contact and with good support around me, I bounced back quicker than I thought I would. I started to date – I realised there were men out there who did like me just the way I was, although I wasn't ready for a relationship and I wasn't ready for casual sex: my heart, while healing, had a long way to go. I wasn't sure I even wanted a relationship with a man ever again.

And that was just fine.

Then one day, quite out of the blue, Big called me to tell me he was leaving Australia.

'I'm at the airport,' he shouted, with the roar of jet engines in the background. 'I'm taking a role in Hong Kong. I can't stay here, Amanda, not without you.'

'Good,' I replied smartly, strongly, bravely. 'Hong Kong is welcome to you.'

Then I hung up and ...

And what?

Burst into tears? Nope. I didn't have any tears left. Jumped with joy? No, I wasn't happy he was gone either. I didn't really feel much at all.

I looked back on the past few years, without the rose-tinted specs. Was our relationship ever that good? Apart from Lake Como and a few nights here and there, a few stolen weekends, was it ever that real? Had he been just a client that I'd fallen in love with? Had I played the whole game wrong? Was it a missed opportunity? I know escorts on retainers with clients who put them up in nice apartments in nice clothes, with a monthly allowance, just like Big. No doubt they still work silently, without their client knowing and feeling no guilt. Why couldn't I have done that? Why did I let my feelings and emotions get in the way? Why couldn't my heart have closed off? Did I really want to be accepted by his friends and family? Did I really, deep down, want to be part of the world of someone who wouldn't accept me for who I truly was?

I spoke to other women in this industry, ones who have husbands and partners, ones who go to work and come back to a normal household with dinner to make and washing to do.

'Don't you fight?' I asked an escort who has been married to her husband for years while working.

'Sure!' she replied. 'We fight! We fight like any other couple. But we fight about stupid stuff, not my job. He gets it. It took him a while to realise it really is just a job, but he gets it.'

Another time, over Champagne in a bustling hotel bar, I asked an escort which would she choose: a relationship or her job?

'I wouldn't choose,' she smiled, clinking my glass. 'You can have both, you know. Imagine that, Samantha. Wouldn't it be nice if you could have both?'

In fact, any time I met with an escort, I would always ask about her love life. It amazed me the ones who were happily coupled, living in bliss. There were also plenty of men who used up the money their girlfriends earned as a way of 'dealing with it'. Sadly, I heard of many women funding their partners' lifestyles out of guilt for working. But in the mix there were men who could accept it without draining the woman's conscience – and bank balance – dry. Not all, but it was possible, wasn't it?

I also realised that this job, this line of work, is almost impossible to give up – certainly harder than I first thought. I thought love would rescue me, that leaving this job would be easy once I'd found love. That being in love was the thing that could kill Samantha. Being fit to be loved, that is.

How wrong I was. The force, the pull of fast cash and easy hours, was stronger, harder, more important than love.

Although there were plenty of understanding and patient partners out there who got that really it was just a job, there were just as many – if not more – women out there who knew they could never stop no matter what their loved ones wanted.

'I keep promising my boyfriend I'll stop when we get engaged, but I'm already planning how to keep working without him finding out,' admitted one. We both laughed. We both understood.

Another confessed to me that her boyfriend found out about her job and she stopped working, suddenly and with a huge pang of guilt. But that lasted two weeks before she started sneaking around again.

'I feel really guilty, but I can't help it,' she lamented. 'The cash is too good. Where else can I make that much money? How can I give it up? I can't! Not even for Alex ...'

That's why when young women come to me, their youthful eyes bright at the thought of becoming an escort, I always warn them of the pitfalls of this industry.

'Relationships will be hard and you get addicted,' I always warn, instead urging them to get a career, get married, have kids first, before they fall under the intoxicating spell of sex work: fast cash and sweet freedom. There is always a price to pay; there is always a cost.

Most women, however, are defiant that they will never stop for a man.

'I'll stop when I want to stop!' said one of my girlfriends in Melbourne.

'Really, when will that be?' I asked, intrigued.

'Oh god, I don't know! Never!' And again, more laughter. Because we understood.

And as my very first madam, Nina, warned me in my first week as a sex worker, in the plush penthouse in North Sydney, to 'never give up for a man', she also warned me never to fall in love with a client. I did both, almost. God bless her: Nina was always right. A woman shouldn't have to give up anything for a man. It will never work. Even Big knew that, deep down.

You need to give up something because *you* want to give it up, not because everyone else wants you to. Just like smoking or drinking, or eating too many cream cakes. You can't give up because someone else doesn't like it. You have to do it for *you*. And if you don't want to stop, it doesn't matter how many times you hear that it's awful and terrible and it will kill you, or how many times you sit in a therapist's chair – you won't stop.

But that was okay. And I was okay with being Samantha. I didn't want a bloody boyfriend anyway. Big had scared me away from love. *Pah!* All that hurt, pain and anger? All that insecurity? Is that love? No, thanks, I'll stick with Samantha until the day I die.

I went to Melbourne, but this time to stay with Tab.

'I need to concentrate on working and saving as much money as I can,' I told her at the kitchen table, popping a piece of orange and poppy-seed cake in my mouth.

'Thank GOD, Amanda!' she replied, putting her plate down, and we hugged, like sisters, with her happy that she finally had her friend back and me happy just because I loved her.

***

Tab wasn't the only one who was delighted that I was back to my old self. So were my clients: Mark, Mr Nice, M from New Zealand, Joe Bananas ...

'It's nice to see you smiling again, darling,' Mark said once as we were taking our seats in the theatre.

'No more problems?' Bananas asked, concerned, just before he flipped me over onto all fours. 'Tell him from me to –'

'No need, Bananas,' I interrupted, parting my legs. We didn't need another line from *The Godfather Part II*. 'He's gone. I'm finally free.'

And Mr Nice, of course, was extremely nice about it.

'I am so happy you're happy,' he grinned before taking a huge slug of shiraz. 'I don't like seeing my ladies upset. No lady deserves that.'

'Good riddance – he sounded like a dickhead,' snorted M over our lukewarm arancini and cold Champagne in the same bar in the same hotel. 'Mind you, for purely selfish reasons, Samantha, I really hope you don't fall in love with anyone else.'

Professor Peter Pan was none the wiser, really, because I hadn't wanted to break his heart and tell him much about Big in the first place. It would no doubt have sent my little psycho into a spin – and you and I both know he had a planet to save.

So yep, things were back on track.

My lovely clients had stuck by me – Mark even took me away to a desert island for a week in the sun.

'You've had a stressful year, darling, and you need a break,' he said, emailing me details of the six-star luxury resort.

We lay by the pool, we fucked on a sand bank, we drank chilled white wine and ate freshly caught seafood. To all the other guests, we could have been a couple.

Like me and Big.

Mark and I watched the sun go down at dusk with cocktails, and we often watched it go up again at dawn, drinking fresh coffee in bed.

Mark was wonderful company, as he always is; he pulled my chair out before I sat down, and gave me space to rest and relax alone during the day. He booked massages for me and brought me chilled water by the pool.

But he wasn't Big.

I really tried, but it was hard not to think about Lake Como.

It was hard not to remember the love Big and I had made on twisted sheets of finest Egyptian cotton; the limoncello we drank until our cheeks flushed; the band that played the samba that swayed us so gently to our sweet sleep.

It was hard not to think about the times in bed when I'd wrapped myself around his body, trying to climb inside.

It was, simply, hard not to think about Big.

I told you that dating me isn't easy. I know that being in love with an escort can really hurt.

But so can loving a client.

As holidays do, mine with Mark came to an end. Relaxed and tanned, he pecked me on the cheek at the airport, put me in a taxi and off we went on our separate ways.

Is Big thinking of me? I couldn't help wondering.

But as time rolled by, and Samantha was picking up more clients again, I started thinking about touring other countries. Could I triple my wage in Europe? Could I make a fortune in London? Other girls were doing it – why couldn't I? Samantha was gathering speed ... I might as well cash in. I knew it wasn't going to last forever. Or was it? Not that it really mattered to anyone else. I had made a promise that I was never going to get involved emotionally with a man for a very long time. If at all.

I couldn't remember where I was going this time – was it Perth or Canberra? One of the two. My suitcase was packed, my lingerie neatly folded in a linen bag tucked away under my high heels and hair dryer.

Now, where was my diary? I couldn't forget that – it had all my bookings in it! What was it? Grant tonight, then Richard tomorrow. Did Simon confirm? Did Alex cancel? I couldn't remember. I'd check at the airport.

Shit, had I packed my charger? Was my toothbrush there? I'd better book my Uber – at that time of day Sydney traffic was a nightmare. Why did I always book my flights in rush hour? When would I ever learn?

Knock knock.

Someone was at the door.

'Bloody hell, Alice!' I yelled over Rosie's bark.

'What took you so long? She's been dying for a walk!' I opened the door, not looking up. 'Go on, Rosie! Out you go!'

'Amanda.'

My head jerked up. Big?

He was standing there, with huge dark circles under his desperate eyes. He looked tired and stressed, and most of all sad.

'I can't live without you.'

He sounded pained.

I quickly tried to slam the door, spluttering and shocked, but his boot was quick to wedge it open.

'Please,' he said. 'I love you. Let me come back. I've accepted it, okay? I don't like it, but I've accepted who you are. I can accept Samantha, however long she hangs around for. But I just want Amanda. I just want *you*.'

I looked at his face – that face I loved so much but also hated. I could smell his smell that I loved but also hated. His nice shoes, nice jeans, big hands that used to wrap neatly around my waist. I felt a prickle of desire, a feeling of lust.

So what now? I loved this man. I loved him for all his imperfections. I am hardly perfect either. I am not an easy person; I know that.

But I hated him too. He'd hurt me. We'd both hurt each other.

No. I couldn't go back. Never go back, I always said that. How long would it be before the same old fights reared their ugly heads? How long before I was nervously checking my phone? Or worrying about which escorts he was sleeping with now? Tab would kill me. My clients would kill me. Samantha would kill me.

Big.

CHAPTER 28

AMANDA

Back on top

The email from my publisher was, as far as emails can be, pretty firm.

Hi Amanda,

We all loved and laughed our way through your book! Well done! But we just need one last chapter. It's not like we don't love the ending of your book, but I think the readers will want to know what happened next. You just need to satisfy them a bit more at the end.

Hi Sophie,

Thanks for your email. I thought we could do that in book three? That way the readers will be dying to know what happened next? Or we could do another chapter in the second print ...?

Hi Amanda,

Great idea but no, you can't leave them hanging like that with Big. We just need 2000 or so words, about anything you like, doesn't have to be about Big. By Monday please! Thank you!

Hi Sophie,
No problem.

Shit.

There was no point in feebly arguing with my publisher. Her word was final, and far more experienced than mine when it came to book writing and things like 'what readers need'.

But the thing is, I'm ashamed to tell you the truth of how it ends. I wanted to end the book leaving you wondering, *What happened to Mr Big? You deserve to be loved, Samantha!*

You see, dear reader, there are things that happened in the course of our relationship that I have been far too embarrassed to tell you about. Silly, really, because I have been so honest about everything else. But despite me protecting his identity, I wanted to protect his integrity too.

'Don't worry, I won't tell them about everything,' I kept reassuring Big over dinner, during sex, whatever we were still doing together. 'I won't tell them about a few things you have done. I don't want my readers to hate you. You will sound mad!'

So perhaps, if I were honest – I were *really* honest – I would tell you the truth. And I would leave him. If I made it public, if I saw the words in black and white, it would give me the strength to leave. If I tell the truth not just to you but to me, I would leave.

I would tell you the truth about him recently looking me in the eyes and telling me he had been diagnosed with a brain tumour. 'I have eight years left maximum,' he told me over dinner at our favourite Italian place. My tears fell into my linguine and he didn't try to wipe them away. He looked at me, cold and emotionless. 'Doctors tell me it is inoperable.'

When I asked him questions, he shut me down.

'I don't want to talk about it,' he said. 'Eat your pasta.'

A few days later, after I pushed for evidence, he reluctantly admitted to me that he had lied.

'To see how much you cared for me. It is your fault I lie, Amanda. This is all your fault.'

See? I put up with that. I put up with that because I felt I didn't deserve any better. I was, after all – as he kept reminding me – a 'tragic hooker'.

'No one else will want you,' was his line. And over the years, the years of Mr Big, I believed him.

And there are other truths – of course there are. But there are also some lines I won't cross. Some secrets I won't betray … Not even my own.

So as I am writing this, he is in my kitchen cooking me pasta amatriciana from scratch. I can hear the garlic sizzling in the Le Creuset pan he bought me, the knife hitting the chopping board expertly. The TV is on full blast (some footy show) and I can hear him calling out to my dogs, Rosie and Georgie, throwing scraps of meat into their eager mouths. It's taken him a while to warm to my dogs, but now he even pats dogs we see in the street.

I am in my bed with a nice glass of red that he has just given to me.

'Is this pinot?' I ask.

He laughs. 'No, darling, it's a special blend. You know nothing about wine, do you!'

I am picking at a little antipasto plate he just made for me: hot salami, roasted eggplant, olives and grissini from the

Italian deli down the road. He doesn't like me too skinny; he likes feeding me. And I like it when he looks after me.

My face is still glowing from the love we just made. His shoes and clothes are neatly folded on his suitcase, and there is a bag on my bedroom floor – a gift he bought me today, a personalised bag.

'I got you a cream one, you have too much black,' he'd said as he passed the beautiful bag to me.

I know tomorrow he goes back to Melbourne, to a life I am not part of. And I go 'on tour' for a couple of weeks as Samantha. I know he will get angry and jealous, and I know I will get suspicious about what he will get up to as well. But now I don't lie to him. Samantha has to work. He knows that. And I know the truth too.

He's promised me that he has changed. But just the other day I found out that he is still paying for sex. He sneaks appointments into his working day to have sex with nameless, faceless women in units near his office. He denies it.

'I am over that stage in my life, darling, you need to believe me,' he keeps saying. But I hear about it from other escorts. He uses different names. Still booking GFE with a 'twist' of PSE. The girls think he's okay, but more to the point, he pays well, he's a good client. Sadly, I think that money … well, it's all he's got.

I've tried to leave him countless times. I've been with other men and told him about it, trying to force him away. But he wears me down. He contacts my family, my friends, people who are close to him. He even started emailing Vanessa.

'I can't ever commit to you, Big,' I keep saying to him. 'I can't ever forgive or forget the lies you've told me and the hurt you've put me through.'

'The past is the past,' he keeps saying back.

We went to the park today to walk the dogs. He grabbed my hand as we walked back to my car.

'If I bought you a ring, an engagement ring of sorts, would you wear it?' he asked, pulling me close to him.

'Really! An engagement ring? And will your kids still be none the wiser? You're so weird, Big ...' And I squeezed out any excitement about what-might-be with grim reality.

But ... a ring! What a joke. Next he will be trying to get me pregnant on the side. It seems clear to me now how men have secret lives, secret wives, secret families. I remember once reading in some newspaper about a firefighter who died on September 11 and how his wife was stunned to discover, after his death, that he had a secret second wife and secret kids. *Incredible*, I remember thinking at the time.

Not so incredible now.

So, yes, I know I shouldn't let this man back into my home, my life. The odds are stacked against us. No one really knows about me in his life, and while everyone knows about him in my life, not many approve. They've seen me cry too many times now.

But nights like tonight – pure and simple domestic bliss – are what I really crave. It's these precious moments of normality, of a bubbling pasta sauce on the stove, of the TV being on, or hearing him *clump-clump* around my house – stuff you all probably take for granted in your marriages, in your homes. All this stuff makes my fragile heart soar. I can pretend for a few hours that this is a normal relationship, that I am being loved by someone who truly loves me.

Except that he doesn't. It's not real. Our relationship isn't real. It's HIRE-A-HUSBAND. Hire some love.

How funny, I feel myself crying now. How silly! Not just crying, sobbing. Real tears.

Big walks in.

'Ready for dinner, Bumbles?' (This is his name for me.) Then he sees my tears. 'What's wrong?'

'It's the last chapter. I don't know why I'm crying.' Sniffing, I wipe my nose on my tracksuit. *I am crying because you need to go. Because your love for me has never been real. I'm crying because I don't know how to leave you.*

'Must be good, then,' he replies, plonking a kiss on my head. 'It must be true, what you're writing. Come on, put the laptop down, dinner's ready.'

I nod, still sniffing. It's time. It's time for him to go.

I watch him eating, with his phone buzzing on the table next to him – top-side down, of course. For a moment, I wish he would choke. I wish a piece of eggplant would get stuck in his throat and I would watch calmly as his terrified eyes stared at me and he grappled for his last breath. But he won't die. What is it they say? Only the good die young.

So here it is. My final chapter, my final words. For now, there is nothing more to say. For *now*. Samantha's life isn't over yet – that I know for sure. She's come too far to give it all up.

There is one person who needs some attention now. She needs some love. And she's been looking in the wrong places. She needs to get back on top. And she will – you know she will.

The final word goes to her.

Amanda.

ACKNOWLEDGEMENTS

Thank you to my girl-power team at Hachette, especially publisher Sophie Hamley, editor Sophie Mayfield, and literary agent Tara Wynne at Curtis Brown.

Thank you to Vanessa and her kind family, and my Angels.

Thank you to my beautiful escort friends and clients who gave me the strength to leave; and to Tab and Alice for being there.

And thank you, my dear readers, for your open minds.

Stay true.